# Time and Again

God's Sovereignty in the Lives of Two Bible
Translators in the Philippines

Richard E. Elkins, PhD and
Agnes Lawless Elkins

WestBow
PRESS
A DIVISION OF THOMAS NELSON

Unless otherwise indicated, Scripture quotations are taken from the King James Version of the Bible.

Scripture quotations marked NIV are from The Holy Bible: The New International Version, copyright © 1978 by the International Bible Society. Used by permission of Zondervan Bible Publishers.

WestBow Press books may be ordered through booksellers or by contacting:

WestBow Press
A Division of Thomas Nelson
1663 Liberty Drive
Bloomington, IN 47403
www.westbowpress.com
1-(866) 928-1240

ISBN: 978-1-4497-3065-9 (sc)
ISBN: 978-1-4497-3066-6 (hc)
ISBN: 978-1-4497-3064-2 (e)

Library of Congress Control Number: 2011919673

Printed in the United States of America

WestBow Press rev. date: 11/23/2011

To the loving memory of my late wife, Betty,
and of
David Allen and Jeff Tackett,
two young men, now in Glory, who walked with our Sovereign Lord
and listened to my telling of these stories

# Contents

# Preface

When we finished our work among the Western Bukidnon Manobos, Betty and I moved to the Matigsalug village of Panganan in 1982 and began language learning among those people. By 1988, because of age and health problems, we realized that a younger team should finish the Matigsalug project. So we spent our final years on the field in translation consulting, training Asian translators, and finishing writing projects.

In 1992, we moved to the United States, where I consulted for translation teams working with Native American languages.

Betty and I returned to the Philippines in 2000 to revise the Western Bukidnon Manobo New Testament with Pastor Saturnino Linog for a second printing. A few years later, he expressed his desire to translate the Old Testament into the Manobo language, and we encouraged him to do so.

Amazingly, Pastor Linog completed this translation in three years by using an accurate model version in a local major language. Then other Manobo leaders formed a team to go over his work.

Now I'm checking this translation for punctuation, spelling, meaning, and word usage. I send it back to them in the Philippines via e-mail attachments for proofing. As we work together, I can't help but remember where it all started and how God directed our paths along the way.

When I have shared the stories in this book in church services, Sunday-school classes, and teaching sessions, many people—friends, colleagues, and strangers—have urged me to put them in writing.

These encouragements made me start writing one story after another. As I wrote, I was overwhelmed with the realization of God's sovereignty in orchestrating events in our lives and in the lives of the people to whom we ministered—time and again.

I trust you will be blessed as you read.

Richard E. Elkins
Fall 2011

# Acknowledgements

It goes without saying that stories do not happen without people, but it is also true that the events recorded in these stories could never have happened without the overriding plans and sovereignty of our heavenly Father. He has been the leading actor and orchestrator.

My thanks goes to Bob Chaney of the Summer Institute of Linguistics, who helped with formatting and gave valuable advice.

Special thanks goes to my dear wife, Agnes Lawless Elkins, for using her writing and editing skills to add to and fine-tune this book. Additional thanks goes to her group of professional writers, who critiqued the stories carefully, asking pertinent questions, making suggestions, and giving encouragement: Diana Savage, Marjorie Stewart, Joan Husby, Carolyn Meagher, and Cindi Bennison. Their help was invaluable.

I am also grateful to Diana Savage for using her graphic-design abilities in preparing the final manuscript and photos for publication.

# Introduction

When you know the main themes that govern the social and cultural world of our Western Bukidnon and Matigsalug Manobo friends, you will better understand the stories in this book.

The most important theme is community survival. Supportive themes are appeasing supernatural beings, keeping the peace, interdependence, food production, and community and personal prestige. When Manobo people enhance any of these themes, they are rewarded with prestige. They view prestige as wealth because they find material wealth virtually impossible to keep in their society.

## Supernaturalism

Supernatural power is fundamental to Manobo religious beliefs, their theories and practice of magic, and their worldview. The major concern in supernaturalism is getting along with gods and spirits for the sake of the community.

## Religious Beliefs

The Manobos believe in a supreme being they call God, Owner, Lord, or Creator. They also believe in lesser deities, such as the gods of farming, rain and thunder, wild game, rivers and streams, and warfare.

Their perception of the unseen world also includes myriad spirits. For example, a spirit may influence a human in at least three ways: One is to cause mild insanity. When this happens, a person may be controllable but acts in irrational ways. A man we knew planted vitamin pills in the family garden. People consider this influence a nuisance but do not fear it.

Secondly, a ghoul spirit may cause a person to be uncontrollable and to exhibit a morbid interest in the dead. Manobos believe that a malevolent ghoul spirit lusts for blood, either human or animal. Such a spirit causes sickness and death in order to taste the blood and eat the body of a person who has died. The story, "Medicine to Drive Away a Ghoul Spirit" is an example of this (ch. 6).

Thirdly, a spirit may offer supernatural assistance through a vision or a dream. One of my co-translators, Francisco Polenda, tells how he believes such an offer came to him:

> Two red-skinned men appeared to me one night. I thought I was dreaming, but I hadn't gone to sleep yet. One of them said, "Our datu[1] has sent us. He wants to ask you something."
>
> I answered, "I will come," and I went with them.
>
> As we walked along, our feet were not touching the ground. We seemed to be floating. In a short time, we came to a large house full of beautiful things.
>
> When I entered the house, my companions spoke to someone, "Datu, this is the man you sent for."
>
> At this, a large man sat down. His body seemed to be half red and half white. He said, "I sent to ask you if you would like to become a shaman."
>
> I answered, "I do not want that."
>
> Then he said to his messengers, "Show him all the things he would like to have."
>
> They showed me the many beautiful possessions in that house. Then they brought me back to their datu.
>
> He asked me again, "What do you think? Do you want to become a shaman?"
>
> I answered as I had before, "I do not want that."
>
> Then the datu said, "Take him home."
>
> The two men took me down a wide road in a large town. We left the town and came to a wide lake. One man pointed west and said, "Go on home. This is the way." Immediately, they vanished.
>
> I turned around, but the wide road we had come on had also vanished. I saw only the lake, wide and dark, and I was terrified. On the other side of the lake, I could see the wide road again. I said to myself, *This path must lead through the water.*

---

1    Important leaders among the Manobo and other tribal groups in Mindanao are given the title of *datu*.

I began to walk through the lake. I thought it would be deep, but the water was just below my knees, and only the lower part of my trousers got wet.

I crossed the lake, came out on the shore, and looked around. The lake had vanished, but the sole of my right foot itched. When I looked down, I saw that a large leech full of blood had attached itself to me. I scraped it off, and my foot bled profusely. Then I seemed to awaken, but I felt sure I had not been dreaming because I hadn't gone to sleep.

I woke my wife and asked her to light a lamp. In the lamplight, I noticed that my foot was bleeding and my trouser legs were wet. It was just before dawn, so I told my wife to cook an early breakfast. Since we were in our field house, I said, "Let's go back to the village. I am frightened by an amazing experience I just had." And I told her what I had seen.

A shaman is a central figure in Manobo religious activities. People rely on him to see into the unseen world, to practice divination, to manipulate, and to appease gods and spirits for the benefit of the community. A shaman's fame and following is the result of his success in solving problems instigated by supernatural beings. People believe he possesses power because he has a supernatural patron who acts for him and speaks through him. A shaman, like a datu, is a peacekeeper, but his peacekeeping has to do with relations between humans and supernatural beings.

Manobos believe that a human is made up of body, breath, and soul. The soul can see, hear, and feel things the body cannot sense, and it even possesses supernatural power. It is responsible for that person's actions and is active in dreams and after death. When a person dies, his body returns to the earth, his breath returns to God, and while journeying to the Golden Home, his soul walks on a narrow bridge over a dark lake filled with fearsome creatures.

In addition, they believe that a deceased person's soul has power to influence people still living. If a soul becomes lonely, it may attempt to take one or more family members to the Golden Home by causing sickness and death. For this reason, the family asks a shaman to perform elaborate rituals, often including animal sacrifices, to keep souls from harming those still living. See "An Interrupted Sunday-School Lesson" for an example of this (ch. 28).

## Magic

According to the Manobo worldview, the power in religion is personal because it involves interaction between humans and supernatural beings. On the other hand, the power in magic is impersonal because it involves the manipulation of impersonal supernatural forces.

By this magic, actions in the ordinary world can have similar but powerful effects in the supernatural realm. For instance, during a funeral, members of the dead person's family cut a strand of Manila hemp that has been attached to the corpse. By this act, they "cut off" his or her soul to prevent it from causing sickness or harm.

## Worldview

In the Western Bukidnon Manobo view, the habitable earth is a round, flat space that includes the island of Mindanao and its environs. Nearby Mount Kalatungan is the center or "navel" of the earth, and their territory is central to all else in the world. To them the sky is a solid dome that rests on the outer rim of the earth. An unseen cosmos overlaps it. Dead souls live in the invisible Golden Home here on earth.

# Peacekeeping

Until the latter half of the last century, the civil government wasn't able to provide services in remote areas for keeping peace and order. Instead, traditional marriage-alliance and litigation systems have minimized violence and settled disputes for centuries.

## The Marriage-Alliance System

When a Manobo man marries, he, with the help of family members, must pay bride wealth to his bride's father and mother. A marriage creates an alliance with strong ties of obligation between the kindred of the groom and the kindred of the bride. A man's obligation to his parents-in-law is a social imperative, and he is never free from it until his father-in-law, his mother-in-law, and certain other members of his wife's kindred are dead.

The relationship of marriage to peacekeeping is obvious because in a sizable community, there are dozens of stable marriage alliances between kindreds, and in-laws are always allies. So this system discourages any kindred member from committing a violent act against anyone else allied to him or her by marriage. In a given area, dozens of marriage ties crisscross the society, effectively binding it together as a community of allies rather than enemies.

## Litigation

While the marriage-alliance system settles disputes and reprisals, the litigation system settles problems not avoided by marriage alliances. A datu occupies a dual role and is a key figure of the litigation system. He not only settles disputes, but he also is a chief leader and decision maker in his community. As a political figure, his power is directly related to his success in litigation.

A datu earns his status by settling disputes. He does not inherit his title, and no one grants it to him formally. To be successful, he must possess certain characteristics: wisdom, the ability to talk skillfully, and enough knowledge of traditional lore to reinforce his statements with sayings and past examples.

He must also have some access to wealth. Often family members will support him economically in his rise to power and prestige. With such wealth, a datu can finance the settlement of a dispute himself. In doing so, he makes an investment that gives him power and prestige. As his success continues, people recognize that to render allegiance to him is advantageous because he will always extricate them in disputes and keep the peace. At this point, the datu peacekeeper becomes a political leader.

Moreover, a strong datu often has several wives, thus tying him to several communities. Aside from the alliances involved, his wives are necessary for economic reasons. Although his followers may help him prepare and plant slash-and-burn fields (swiddens), the women are the ones who care for the fields afterwards until harvest. Having several wives allows a datu to plant several fields. He then can use the extra food in litigation or invest it to increase his power and prestige.

## Interdependence

Interdependence is vital for group survival. Life was precarious before lowland Filipino culture and government were widespread. Slash-and-burn agriculture was demanding, often unproductive, and could result in famine.

During times of famine, people who acquire food share with others. If a man has an abundant crop, family members who help him harvest can share in the bounty. If they have good crops later, he helps them harvest and shares in their bounty. To refuse to share is unthinkable. In this way, food is distributed throughout the community and adds to the likelihood of survival when food is scarce.

Reciprocity is not limited to food sharing. People also share extensive or laborious tasks. A man who plans to clear a field or build a house may announce his need for assistance. His friends and relatives will help finish the task in a festive manner in a fraction of the time otherwise spent. The man and his family then provide a substantial meal for the workers.

## Food Production

Food production is a constant concern. Slash-and-burn horticulture is arduous, and these people believe that success in producing a reasonable harvest depends as much on proper magic and the cooperation of supernatural beings as it does on diligence and labor.

Rice is the major crop because rice is the epitome of good food. To a Manobo, happiness is having enough rice to eat.

The favorite substitute for rice is corn, which the people dry, shell, and grind in volcanic-stone hand mills. This produces corn grits that they cook and eat like rice. Other staple foods are sweet potatoes, cassava, bananas, and wild yams.

## Community and Personal Prestige

Personal, family, and community prestige are major concerns. In a society where opportunities for economic improvement are sharply limited, it's virtually impossible to move toward a higher economic level.

The only way that Manobo individuals can become "wealthy" is by amassing prestige. For them, prestige and status constitute unseen wealth. The most highly sought-after state is one in which a person, his family members, and his community are widely known and praised. The most feared state is one in which a person, his family, and his community "lose face" because of shameful acts that one or more of them have committed. Thus, the avoidance of shame and the quest for prestige are constant concerns.

Now that you know a little more about the Western Bukidnon and Matigsalug Manobo people, I hope you enjoy the following stories of our experiences. It was an enormous privilege to live and work with these wonderful people on the southern island of Mindanao.

# In the Beginning

## 1941–52

Once summer evening in 1941, when I was at a church youth camp, the speaker's message stirred my heart. I walked back to our cabin with my talkative friends, but I could hardly wait to get alone.

I crawled into my bunk and lay on my back. *Oh, God*, I prayed silently, *I'll be anything you want me to be; I'll do anything you want me to do; I'll go anywhere you want me to go—and I hope it will be to China*. Peace filled my heart, for I felt God had accepted my offer.

A few months prior to this in my freshman year in high school, I had met Elsie Mae Buttles, a woman I'll never forget. She had been a missionary nurse in China with the China Inland Mission but had contracted tuberculosis and had come to our high-desert city, Albuquerque, New Mexico, for treatment. Her doctors told her she could never return to China.

Following Elsie's recovery, she became a nurse in a local hospital. On her day off, she held after-school Bible classes for teenagers. She explained the gospel in such a clear way that I had decided to receive Christ as my Savior and to follow him. That summer she sent me to her church's youth camp where I experienced the joy of fellowship with God and with other Christian young people.

After my World War II service in the Navy, I entered Westmont College in Santa Barbara, California, in 1947. My first morning at breakfast, a beautiful young lady with light-brown hair handed me a bowl of oatmeal as I went through the cafeteria line. The name on her tag intrigued me—Betty Thumlert. I thought, *Some man will certainly change that name.* Since I was shy around girls, I never dreamed I might be the one.

A few weeks later, a dorm friend dared three of us to ask three junior girls for dates. In God's sovereign providence, I asked Betty. Before I came to school, I had decided to focus on my studies and not get seriously involved with a girl. But now—there was Betty. From that time on, I put "the heart before the course." Betty was an amazing young lady. She not only was pretty, amiable, and intelligent, but she had a heart for God. Neither of us had a car, so we got well-acquainted on long walks near the college.

However, one thing about our relationship needed to be addressed. I was headed for the mission field, most likely to some remote corner of the world like China. Betty was a city girl who had never even been camping. Would it be fair to ask her to share my life in such a place? But when I asked her to marry me, she said yes.

A year earlier, her pastor had told her, "Betty, the Lord may never directly call you to serve as a missionary, but he may call you to some young man whom he has called. If that happens, you must never look back." Thankfully, she took his counsel seriously. We married in 1949 after Betty graduated. She took a job as a receptionist in a local medical facility, and I continued my studies.

By then, China was closed to missionaries because of the Communist takeover, so we asked God to lead us to another field. During those years, several men from Wycliffe Bible Translators spoke in chapel, and they challenged us about the need for Bible translation around the world. I realized I had a flair for languages because I was learning to speak Spanish, and I enjoyed Dr. Charles Ryrie's Greek classes. So Betty and I decided we would like to become Bible translators.

I graduated in January 1951, and we applied to the Summer Institute of Linguistics training program at the University of Oklahoma. In February, Betty's mother died, and we borrowed money to fly to Seattle for her funeral.

While there, Betty's pastor, the Rev. Forrest Johnson of Tabernacle Baptist Church, encouraged us to consider working with the Association of Baptists for World Evangelism (ABWE) rather than with Wycliffe. He suggested we attend an ABWE conference in Oakland, California, in May and begin the process of becoming members. A couple in his church even gave us money so we could go.

However, the week before the ABWE conference, my mother in Albuquerque became ill and died. We quit our jobs in California, put our belongings in storage, and left for New Mexico. We returned the money to the couple in Seattle. We still felt we should at least get the language training Wycliffe offered. But we were in debt, and we had no money for school that summer. I looked for a job in Albuquerque but found none.

When I came home one evening after job hunting, Betty met me at the door with light in her eyes and a large manila envelope. Inside were seven-hundred-dollars worth of matured war bonds her mother had bought and made payable to her. The amount was enough to settle our debts and cover our summer studies.

At the University of Oklahoma at Norman, we entered the intriguing world of linguistics—phonetics, phonemics, verb morphology, and descriptive grammar. For practice, we learned how to discover grammar patterns in languages, such as Quechua, Aztec, Machiguenga, and Turkish. A taste of missionary anthropology and cross-cultural communications finished the course.

While we were at the university, we met Howard and Bobie McKaughan. They also were friends of Dr. Charles Ryrie, my professor and friend at Westmont College. Howard and Bobie invited us to join them for a weekly lunch with members of the first group of translators going to the Philippines. As time passed, we shared a deepening feeling that God wanted us in Wycliffe.

During one of his chapel talks, Dr. Kenneth Pike, a leader in linguistics and Bible translation, said, "If you are going to play a game, the *field* you play on is not nearly as important as the *team* with which you play." That clinched it for us. We felt God wanted us to join these remarkable people who were going to the Philippines to begin Bible translation for many of the more than 170 languages spoken in that island nation.

We returned to Albuquerque in the fall. For the second time in four months, we were without funds, but it didn't matter. We were members of Wycliffe Bible Translators and the Summer Institute of Linguistics (SIL), Wycliffe's primary partner that conducts field operations in various parts of the world. And we were excited to be part of the first team going to the Philippines. When we looked back, we understood that God used the deaths of both our mothers to lead us to join Wycliffe and SIL.

Pastor Johnson was not happy with our decision. The next time we saw him, he said, "I know you feel strongly that God has led you, but down deep in my heart I can't help feeling that God wants you in Bukidnon [a province in the Philippines] standing shoulder to shoulder with our ABWE missionaries."

Later, on our first furlough, I reminded him of his remark and said, "Pastor Forrest, you were right. That is exactly where God led us, and we work in Bukidnon near Ron and Davy Esson, Dr. Lincoln and Lenore Nelson, and their fellow missionaries in ABWE."

Our next step was an orientation course held in eastern Oklahoma, then we spent three months at Wycliffe's jungle camp in the rain forests of Chiapas in southern Mexico. We hiked for miles, slept in jungle hammocks, cooked over open fires, and learned to cope in primitive cultures.

The training was tough but invigorating. We felt ready for anything.

# 2

# God and a Briggs-and-Stratton Engine

# 1952

After jungle camp in the spring of 1952, Betty was pregnant with our first child, so she rested for several weeks at our organization's headquarters in Mexico City.

Meanwhile, George Cowan, the director, sent me on a bus to the state of Oaxaca to join translator John Crawford in a dialect survey of the Mixe Indian region. The pilot of a Missionary Aviation Fellowship (MAF) plane, E. W. Hatcher or "Hatch," as we called him, picked me up at the linguistic center in Mitla near Oaxaca City, and we flew eastward over the mountains toward the Mixe area.

When Hatch began the descent sometime later, I saw what looked like a postage-stamp-size clearing on a mountainside.

"That's Totontepec!" Hatch shouted over the noise of the engine, and the plane settled down into the approach, landing safely.

John Crawford, his wife Gwen, and their small son met us. Gwen was expecting their second child, so she and their youngster flew back with Hatch. I was to accompany John on a hiking trip to survey and record the dialect differences of Mixe speakers of the area. This task is often necessary before the work of Bible translation begins.

We spent the next several weeks trekking from village to village through beautiful mountainous country where the trails were either straight up or straight down. John recorded language data in each village. I found the hiking demanding, even though I was in fairly good shape from our earlier jungle-camp experience. John planned the survey so that the last village to visit was on the western edge of the language area and halfway back to Mitla. From there, we would walk the final thirty miles.

By early May, we had spent a month on the survey and arrived at the last village one late afternoon. Besides John's books, papers, and linguistic data, we had our sleeping gear and clothes. Our effects were heavy, so we had hired carriers in each village to take us to the next village. As soon as we arrived, the carriers set down their loads, received their pay, and started back over the trail for home. They would walk most of the way in the dark.

John led the way to the *municipio*, the town office, where he found the town secretary. A few bystanders looked on suspiciously while John explained why we had come and where we were going.

The secretary responded with obvious hostility. "Señor, the dialect here is just the same as it is where you live in Totontepec. We have no place for you to spend the night or find any food. We suggest you continue your journey immediately to the next village."

This was surprising because people in other villages either welcomed us cordially or expressed no more than casual indifference. For some reason, local authorities seemed suspicious of our presence in the area.

I prayed silently, *Lord, how are you going to get us out of this? These people are hostile. We can't go on tonight in the dark nor can we carry our equipment by ourselves. And the next village is a six-hour walk away!*

As we stood there, John noticed a small Briggs-and-Stratton gasoline engine on the porch of the municipio. He turned to the secretary. *"Pues, señor, que tiene la maquina?"* ("Sir, what is wrong with the engine?")

"Oh, señor, it is completely out of order. It runs the generator for the lights in the town plaza. The town elders are devastated because we will be forced to hire six men to carry it into Mitla to be repaired. This will be very expensive."

John, the man of the hour, smiled. "Well, señor, I am something of a mechanic. Would you like me to look at it?" Actually, John was more than "something" of a mechanic. He was an automobile buff and had considerable skill with engines.

The secretary's countenance brightened. "Oh, señor, would you please see if you can repair it?"

John and I walked over to the engine. He made preliminary tests and found that the needle valve was totally out of adjustment. He gave it the proper number of turns then pulled on the starter cord. The engine came to life with a roar. After further adjustments, he shut off the motor and started it again. We carried it to its concrete base near the generator and bolted it down. Then we attached the generator belt to the engine, and John pulled the starter cord again. The lights in the plaza glowed dimly at first, then brightly. John asked others to stop and start the engine by themselves so they would know he had not used witchcraft or magic.

It was dark by this time, but the cheerful glow of the plaza lights lifted our spirits. John was still leaning over the engine when the secretary tapped him on the shoulder. "Señor, your supper is ready. You will sleep here inside the municipio tonight. I will be glad to teach you anything you want to know about the language." Then he added, *"Estan los ancianos muy encantados con la vida.* ("The elders are very enchanted with life.") Tomorrow we are sending six men to accompany you and carry your effects to Mitla."

In a few moments, our sovereign God had used John and an out-of-adjustment engine to transform us in the eyes of the townspeople from unwanted intruders to friends. They gave us a good supper of fragrant corn tortillas, beans, and chili, then showed us where we could lay out our sleeping gear.

The next day's trek was long. We left at seven in the morning and reached Mitla in the dark at ten o'clock that night. John took our traveling companions to the marketplace, bought them supper, and offered them pay, which they took reluctantly.

We were both exhausted, but we praised the Lord. It was a good lesson in faith for me, a neophyte would-be Bible translator, soon to be hiking the hills of Mindanao in the Philippines.

Today, many years and many trodden Philippine miles later, I think back on those good days with John and the wonderful people in the beautiful mountains of eastern Oaxaca, and I am grateful to God. I also am *muy encantado con la vida* ("very enchanted with life").

# 3

# Song from a Sawhorse
## 1952–54

After the survey trip with John Crawford, I joined Betty in Mexico City, and we returned to New Mexico, where our daughter Kathleen was born on June 13, 1952.

We spent a second summer in linguistic studies, this time with a baby, at the University of North Dakota in Grand Forks. In the fall months, we visited potential prayer-and-financial partners.

During January and February of 1953, we stayed with my father in Albuquerque. I worked for a plumbing company until our visas had been approved. In March we sailed on a British freighter for the Philippines.

A few weeks after our arrival in Manila, our director, Dr. Richard Pittman, assigned us to work with one of the Manobo languages on the southern island of Mindanao. Since other linguists also were going south, we men went ahead on a steamer through the many islands and set up temporary headquarters in Musuan, Bukidnon Province. Our wives and children followed by plane a few days later.

Our adventures were to begin at last. We were more than ready to put into practice all we had learned in our linguistic courses and in our jungle-camp training.

On a bright April morning, Jim Dean, Dick Pittman, and I drove over gravel, "washboard" roads to find a place where Betty and I could study the Manobo language. On a previous visit, Dr. Pittman learned that a number of Manobo families lived in and near the village of Damulog among families who spoke Visayan, the trade language in the area.

We drove through pristine rain forests and a number of small villages then picked up a man who agreed to show us his rental house. When we reached Damulog, we talked to the local leader of the Manobo people, Datu Hilarion Managkil.[2] After we explained our purpose, we walked to the two-story house built of weathered split boards, and my heart sank. Cockroaches scurried away when we entered, and rat droppings gave evidence of a colony hidden in the corners. The floor had missing boards, and a large log with notched steps led the way upstairs through a jagged hole in the ceiling.

Dick Pittman struck a corner post with his fist, and the whole house trembled. He smiled at the landlord. "That's a real sturdy post," he said.

I had my doubts. We had been trained to pioneer, and we were going to have an opportunity to test our mettle.

"How much is the rent?" Dick asked.

The landlord cocked his head. "Mmm, ten pesos a month ($5.00 US)—that is, if certain repairs are made on the house."

Dick Pittman nodded. "Oh, repairs are no problem. Mr. Elkins is an expert carpenter."

I smiled to myself. Friends in the United States had given me a good set of tools, but my woodworking skills left much to be desired.

Final details were worked out, and we returned to Musuan. Before long, fellow missionary, Bus Dawson, and I returned to Damulog to secure the doors and make other repairs. Later, Betty, Kathleen, our ten-month-old daughter, and I moved in, and we were on our own.

Datu Managkil sent Lumundao Dalas, a small, meek-looking man, to help us learn to speak Manobo. Mr. Dalas had been a schoolteacher before World War II and could speak English.

"I'm willing to spend time each day to teach you the language," he said, "but I really need a full-time job."

I grinned. "It's wonderful that you'll be our teacher. If you can use my tools to repair the house and make us some rough furniture, we'll hire you on a daily basis."

He agreed, and we began language study.

After our early enthusiasm wore off, life became difficult. Betty and I could barely cope with menial tasks. Since we were seven degrees from the

---

2    Important leaders among the Manobo and other tribal groups in Mindanao are given the title of *datu.*

equator, the weather was hot and sticky. We had to carry our water from a nearby spring. People made demands on us that we didn't know how to meet. We were perplexed, depressed, and thought we'd go crazy listening to a guitar next door droning on and on in a minor key. Even the sun-filled sky seemed dark. We didn't admit it to each other, but we were both experiencing culture shock and responded by having a pity party.

One morning as we tried to work on language data, I felt sorry for myself and prayed silently, *Lord, I think you've made a terrible mistake. This really isn't what I had in mind when I volunteered to be a missionary. I don't like this place, and I don't think much of these people, either.*

Suddenly, the silence was broken by someone singing—in English! It seemed to come from the backyard.

> Softly and tenderly Jesus is calling, calling for you and for me;
> See, on the portals He's waiting and watching, watching for you and for me.
> Come home, come home, ye who are weary, come home;
> Earnestly, tenderly, Jesus is calling, calling, O sinner, come home![3]

I scrambled down the notched log ladder and ran out the door. There, sawing away, was Mr. Dalas singing, "Come home; come home, ye who are weary, come home." Going "home" was exactly what I wanted to do.

He stopped sawing when he saw my astonished face, and I sat down on the sawhorse. "Lumundao," I asked, "where did you learn that song?"

"I learned it many years ago when I was baptized."

I was stunned. "Do you know why we have come to live here and study the Manobo language?"

He wrinkled his brow. "No, I don't know why you have come. Everyone is wondering why Americans like you would want to live in this place."

I smiled. "God has sent us here to learn Manobo so someday we can translate the Word of God into your language. Then your people can read it for themselves in words they clearly understand."

Lumundao's eyes filled with tears. "This is the hand of God!" he said. "For many years I have prayed that my people might have God's Word in our language."

Suddenly, the sun shone brighter, the guitar next door struck major chords, and my spirits lifted. We were right on track! In his infinite

---

3    "Softly and Tenderly, Jesus Is Calling," by Will L. Thompson.

wisdom, God had brought us to this village, to Lumundao Dalas, to the Manobo people. The only believer among thousands of Manobos was in our backyard sawing and singing to bring comfort and joy to two new, disheartened missionaries.

We had a good year in Damulog. With Lumundao's patient help, we progressed in the language and became familiar with Manobo culture. We thoroughly enjoyed our many new friends. When we moved further into the interior, we could communicate and make our way through the cultural maze of a totally Manobo community.

But we never forgot Lumundao, the quiet little man whose song made an unexpected difference during difficult days for two green and lonely would-be Bible translators.

# 4

# Rain-Forest Surgery

## 1953

Betty and I had been living in the village of Damulog only a few months when Datu Managkil sent us a note: "Please send me medicine for bleeding. A wild pig bit my nephew."

I assumed that his nephew was a child who had tangled with a feral pig in the rain forest. "It can't be too serious," I said to Betty, "if all he wants is medicine." But I didn't know what medicine might be specifically for bleeding, and I was sure we didn't have any.

I approached my language teacher, Lumundao. "Do you know where these people live?"

"Yes, in a clearing in the rain forest."

In our previous jungle-camp training in Mexico, we'd had classes in first aid and tropical diseases, so we could treat people with simple remedies and basic antibiotics. I packed a bag with bandages, antibiotic ointment, and the items needed to give a shot of penicillin. I was glad that most pharmacies in the Philippines carried such supplies.

Lumundao and I said good-bye to Betty then hiked into the shady gloom of the rain forest. Soon we came to a large pool fed by a creek.

Lumundao gazed into the dark water. "He isn't dead yet."

"How do you know?"

"This pool is called *Kirembis,* 'Place of the worn-out sleeping mat.'"

I was puzzled. "Why do people call it that?"

"It is local belief that when someone has just died, the spirit of the pool displays a worn-out mat floating in the water."

I had lived there long enough to know that I had to abandon my Western skepticism, so I was not surprised. It was just another example of the importance of supernaturalism in that culture—a belief in "something out there" that most people are unaware of in our society. Over time, I realized that Satan often acts supernaturally to support a local worldview, and this one seemed truthful to my Manobo friends.

We hiked on and soon came to an extensive, newly cut clearing in the forest. In the center stood a large temporary structure used as a storeroom and a shelter from the weather during the growing and harvesting season. A number of people were gathered outside. Inside we found a young man lying on a sleeping bench. A dirty turban holding what looked like cotton batting was wrapped around his upper torso.

"What happened?" I asked the datu.

"My nephew, Sinapew, was on a pig hunt with a group of men and dogs. When the dogs cornered a large wild boar, he threw his spear and missed." He explained that the pig charged Sinapew, knocked him down, slashed him with its long sharp tusks then gored him in the abdomen.

I looked uneasily at the makeshift bandage. "May I open this to see what needs to be done?"

"Yes, open it."

Untying the bandage, I saw a deep slash angling from his lower right abdomen almost to his armpit. The opening had been stuffed with pieces of kapok. *This is not for me,* I thought as I tied him up again. *I'll have to see if Dr. Linc will come.*

Dr. Lincoln Nelson, medical missionary with the Association of Baptists for World Evangelism (ABWE), lived a five-hour bus ride from us in the provincial capital of Malaybalay. Following service as a naval surgeon in World War II, Dr. Nelson had come to the Philippines with his family a year before to begin a remarkable medical evangelistic work that has continued for more than fifty years.

It was already late afternoon. If I caught the five o'clock bus the next morning, I might be able to get Linc to come back with me in time to save the young man's life.

I cleaned and bandaged a slash on the patient's leg and gave him a shot of penicillin. Before we left, I told the people gathered around that I would try to get a doctor to come and care for Sinapew.

Lumundao and I set out on the path to return to our village. When we reached the pool, he again peered at it. "Still no worn-out mat floating," he said.

Early the next morning, a Sunday, I boarded the bus and asked the driver, a friend of mine, "Can you drive a little faster today? A man might die if I don't get to Malaybalay in a hurry." The driver usually took five hours to make the trip since he picked up passengers, but that morning he made it in two.

As the bus came down the hill toward a bridge outside of town, I saw Dr. Linc driving toward us in his jeep. I called to the driver, "Stop on the bridge, and block the doctor's way!"

I jumped out of the bus and ran to the jeep. "Am I glad to see you!" I said. "Where are you going?"

"To visit a village church today."

"How would you like to take a hike with me instead to save a man's life?"

Linc grinned. "Why not?"

I thanked the bus driver and climbed into the jeep. We turned around and started back to the clinic. On the way, I told Linc about Sinapew's injuries and the need for professional help.

The doctor changed clothes and collected medical and surgical supplies then we were soon on the road again. We stopped in nearby Valencia to pick up Mr. Sinunglay, a local evangelist who spoke some Manobo.

We reached Damulog around noon. Betty quickly prepared lunch for us, and a few minutes later, Lumundao joined us to guide us on the hike back into the forest. When we reached the pool, he peered again into the dark depths and said, "He's still alive."

We pushed on until we came to the clearing.

The patient was alive and conscious.

After a preliminary examination, Dr. Linc turned to me. "Dick, have you ever assisted in a surgery?"

I gulped and shook my head.

"We'll need to set up a clean surgical platform to lay the instruments on."

Someone produced a large empty basket, which we turned upside down. Linc went to the doorway and pointed to several large banana plants nearby with leaf stalks that had not yet unfolded. "Several of those will do," he said.

A man quickly got them. The house was full of curious people, and all were anxious to be at the doctor's beck and call.

Linc and I scrubbed our hands and arms with green soap and put on rubber gloves. He unrolled the large banana leaves and laid them on the basket, spread a sterile cloth on the leaves, and laid out his instruments. He carefully removed the dirty turban and pieces of kapok covering the wound. I held the wound open to allow access to the surgical area while Mr. Sinunglay shined a flashlight. I was amazed at how quickly the doctor worked and how casual he seemed as he cleaned the deep wound, injected an anesthetic, tied off bleeding vessels, and stitched up three torn layers of muscle and skin. Evidently, no vital organs had been damaged.

Soon Linc inserted a drain and closed up the wound. He administered another shot of penicillin, and through Mr. Sinunglay, he gave instructions about further care. We'd brought a stretcher, and Linc told the people they should use it to bring Sinapew to Damulog in two days, where I could give him daily shots of penicillin.

Then Mr. Sinunglay briefly explained the message of salvation through Jesus Christ. I read a few verses in Manobo from the third chapter of the Gospel of John that Lumundao and I had translated.

Before we left, the people thanked us for helping Sinapew. I prayed for them on our hike back. I longed to give them more than physical help, but my ability to speak Manobo was still rudimentary. A New Testament in their language would take many more years of language learning and study.

When we reached Damulog, the good doctor left for home. Two days later, relatives carried Sinapew to our village on the stretcher. I followed Linc's instructions, changed the patient's bandages, and gave him medication for several weeks. He recovered fully but had a long scar across his abdomen as a reminder of his ordeal.

A few months later, just before our son Tom was born, Betty and I left the area to be nearer medical facilities. Then a few weeks after his birth, I returned to Damulog to see how Sinapew was doing. Someone told me he now lived in a large clearing in a valley south of our village. I drove there and asked a man where I might find our former patient.

What happened next was completely unexpected. The man stepped to a spot overlooking the clearing and shouted, "Sinapew, your friend is here!"

The call was relayed several times from house to house until the answer came back, "What friend is that?"

"Your American friend, the one who helped to medicine you!" Like an echo, this too was relayed over the clearing.

Shortly, a smiling, robust Sinapew appeared, and we spent a while in friendly conversation.

I never saw Sinapew again, but I have a spear that once belonged to him. I often show it to friends and tell how many years ago, I assisted Dr. Linc in rain-forest surgery to save Sinapew's life.

# 5

# Bandits Strike Damulog

## 1953–54

One day Lumundao climbed up our notched-log stairs. After greeting us, he warned, "If people you don't recognize come to your house at night, don't let them in."

"Why?" I asked.

"They may be bandits," he explained. "A few weeks ago, Philippine Constabulary soldiers from this province fought with bandits in the next province south of here. They defeated them and killed a number of men. Now we hear that the group plans to seek revenge by attacking our village because we're the largest community on this side of the border. If we receive any more information, I'll let you know so you can leave."

"Thank you. We'll be very careful."

The weeks and months passed with nothing happening, and we almost forgot about Lumundao's warning.

The next May, we awaited the birth of our second child. When the time of delivery drew near, Dr. Lincoln Nelson urged us to move closer to the Bethel Baptist Clinic in Malaybalay. "It's not wise for Betty to remain so far from medical assistance," he said.

We agreed with the good doctor, for the bumpy bus ride on gravel roads to Malaybalay always took five hours.

Some time prior to that, President Zosimo Montemayor of the Mindanao Agricultural College at Musuan, Bukidnon, had offered our organization a house on campus to use as our southern headquarters.

Since the college was not far from Malaybalay, our director, Howard McKaughan, suggested we move to Musuan to represent our organization and wait for the birth of our child.

One morning in late May, we loaded our worldly goods on a hired pickup truck, said good-bye to our friends, and moved to Musuan. Tom was born a month later.

Soon after, a friend from Damulog came to see us. "The day after you left," he said, "the bandits robbed every house and even killed a small boy on his way home from school."

The friend explained that later, on the evening of the robbery, the bus from Malaybalay pulled in to Damulog where the driver and conductor usually spent the night. They had just changed their clothes and were ready for bed when bandits broke in, robbing them both. They even took the conductor's trousers that contained the day's fares. After the bandits left, the driver and conductor drove back to Malaybalay and notified the authorities. They returned later with a detachment of armed constabulary police.

Our friend, Lumundao, approached the police commander. "I think the bandits are spending the night in an empty house in the rain forest some distance away," he said. "If you like, I'll lead you there."

The commander agreed, and the police walked down a dark forest trail for over an hour, led by their skillful Manobo guide. Just after midnight, Lumundao whispered to the commander, "We are at the edge of the clearing. If you agree, I will crawl underneath the house. I understand their language, so I can tell if the bandits are there." The commander motioned his concurrence, and like a phantom, Lumundao silently disappeared into the darkness. A short time later, he reappeared. "I was right!" he whispered. "They are there—all of them!"

When the commander gave an order, his men opened fire at the dark house. Shouts erupted, and the bandits leaped from the structure and fled into the forest.

In a few moments, all was quiet. The officers waited, then moved forward cautiously. When they entered, the house was empty, but blood indicated that some had been wounded. In their frenzied flight, the bandits had left their plunder behind, including the bus conductor's trousers with all the day's fares still in the pocket. Apparently, the bandits had not discovered the money.

Betty and I praised God when we heard this story. Obviously, he had removed us from Damulog just in time. We did not like to think what the effect might have been on Betty in her last month of pregnancy had we been on the scene.

Only God knew that the baby to be born would someday be one of his servants to take the good news to a people group in Mexico that had never heard the gospel.

# 6

# Medicine to Drive Away a Ghoul Spirit

## 1955

While in Musuan, Betty and I decided not to return to Damulog where the Manobo people were a small minority.

Since the end of World War II, many Filipinos from other islands had moved to Damulog in search of land and better lives. Their influence changed the way local Manobo people lived. We needed to find an area where we could learn the language and culture without outside influences. Our search ended when, with the help of Dr. Lincoln Nelson and missionary Ron Esson, we found the inland village of Barandias, inhabited only by Manobos.

Once our family had settled into our new home in Barandias, the local datu recommended that I hire Siblian, a quiet young man next door, as my teacher.

Siblian's education had been interrupted when the Japanese invaded the Philippines during World War II, so he attended school through grade five only. But he had a zest for learning. I taught him English, and he taught me the Manobo language. He borrowed my books and pored over them at night by the light of a smoky kerosene lamp.

After Betty and I spent a couple of years studying the language, I attempted some elementary translation. Siblian and I started with the Gospel of Mark and worked together in the mornings. In the afternoons, I studied the Greek text and commentaries while he worked in the field near his home.

Soon the Scriptures began to affect Siblian. One day we translated the passage where John the Baptist denounced King Herod for taking the wife of his brother Philip (Mark 6:17–19).

Siblian looked up at me. "Is it true that God will forgive our sins?" he asked. "I don't mean just a little sin. I'm talking about something really big."

Later, I discovered that he had stolen his cousin's wife. The Scriptures had convicted him of his sin.

On another morning, we translated Jesus' encounter with the demon-possessed Gerasene man who lived in a graveyard (Mark 5:1–20). That afternoon Siblian came to me. "*Geli*,"[4] he asked, "what is the medicine for a person whose mind has gone away?"

Assuming a friend had a psychiatric problem, I said, "Certain doctors know about that, but I'm afraid I cannot help. Is someone sick like that here?"

"It's Anuy," he said, speaking of a young villager. "He has been out of his mind for several days and is running around like a wild animal. His relatives tied him up in their field, but this morning he broke away. He ran to the burial ground, dug up a child's grave, and pulled out the body. The whole village is terrified!"

"Do you know what that reminds me of?" I asked.

"Of course—what we translated this morning about the man who lived in the burial ground and was afflicted with many ghoul spirits.[5] A ghoul spirit has captured Anuy, and we don't know what to do for him. Do you have any medicine that would help?"

I shook my head. "No, but we must pray to God the Father in the name of Jesus and ask him to drive that evil thing away. God is more powerful than any ghoul spirit, and he can free Anuy from it."

"How do we pray?" Siblian asked.

"We talk to God just like I'm talking to you, but we ask in Jesus' name because he has given us the authority to do that."

"You and Mother of Kathleen[6] pray for Anuy."

---

4    We learned never to address Siblian by his name. Instead, I called him *Geli* (pronounced "Gully"), a term used between males of similar ages.

5    Manobo people believe that evil supernatural beings have an insatiable lust for human flesh and blood.

6    *Mother of Kathleen* was the local teknonym ("name") for Betty. I was called *Father of Kathleen*. The polite way of referring to married people is *father* or *mother* of their eldest child

"You pray, also," I urged.

But Siblian shook his head. He was too deeply entrenched in animistic beliefs, so he did not want to offend a spirit by praying to the Christian God.

That night Betty and I quietly and simply prayed for Anuy, asking God in the name of Jesus to drive the evil spirit away from him.

Early the next morning, our coworkers, Bus and Jane Dawson, arrived in their Jeep with the news that the mission's executive committee planned to hold special meetings at our center at Nasuli. As a committee member, I needed to attend. We packed up and left the village with the Dawsons and our children. But I couldn't help wondering what happened to Anuy, and we kept praying for him.

Six weeks later, we returned to Barandias on a government truck that let us off near the village about 5 p.m. I left Betty and the children with our supplies and walked up the hill to Siblian's house. "Can you please get some men to help carry our baggage?" I asked. He agreed, and I returned to my family in the gathering darkness.

A few minutes later, a group of men came down the path, and Anuy was with them. I studied him carefully to see if he were in his right mind. He seemed okay.

When we arrived home, we lit a pressure lamp and swept up dead cockroaches and rat droppings that had accumulated while we were gone. Betty started to cook a pot of rice, but I said, "I can't wait any longer. I'm going to talk to Siblian."

When I found him, I asked, "What happened to Anuy? The last time we were here, he was captured by a ghoul spirit, and now he seems perfectly normal."

"But you prayed," he answered, "and that very night the spirit left him! He's been fine ever since."

This incident became the chink in Siblian's animistic armor. Later, after he had trusted Christ, he told us that Anuy's deliverance convinced him of the truth of the Bible. "Christ really is more powerful than the ghoul spirits," he said. Anuy also became a Christian and was never again demonized.

This was a tremendous confirmation for Betty and me. God, the Great Orchestrator, delivered Anuy on the very day Siblian and I translated the story of the demoniac of Gerasa. The gospel became relevant to Siblian when he saw Christ's power operating on a real problem in his own world. God proved that his power was indeed greater than that of evil spirits.

Later, Siblian became the local gospel communicator and the tool God used to birth the Manobo church.

# 7

# Incest!

## 1955

Shortly after we came to live with the Manobo people, we learned they observed a strong taboo called *anit* that prohibited talking to animals. People warned us sharply about speaking to our cat or to dogs that roamed the village. Breaking this taboo was *anit*. "This means," one of them said, "that *anit* causes the thunder god, Manewvanew, to become angry, and he will strike someone in the village with lightning."

We quickly sensed that the Manobos considered even a slight infraction of this taboo a serious matter. When we expressed our ignorance about *anit*, people were surprised. "You Americans don't know about *anit*? Surely, everyone all over the world knows about that."

"We've never heard of it," I said. "But because we respect you and your customs, we don't want to cause you anxiety. We promise we won't break the taboo."

At home, Betty and I agreed that we did not want to be blamed if anyone happened to be struck by lightning. Next, we told young Kathleen and Tom, "Don't talk to our cat when the neighbors are around. That frightens them."

As time went by, we discovered other variants of the taboo. One day while a neighbor was plowing a garden spot for us, our three-year-old Tom was in the plowed area picking up earthworms. He carried two tin cans, an empty one and one containing water. He carefully washed the dirt off each worm in the water then placed it in the other can.

Several Manobo women stood with us watching the plowing and, with rather morbid interest, watching Tom.

One woman looked at Betty. "What is your son doing?"

"What are you doing, Tom?" Betty asked.

"Giving these worms a bath."

Betty turned to the women. "He's bathing the earthworms."

*"Ed-anit heeyan!* That will *anit!"*

I quickly took the worms away from Tom. "What you're doing frightens these people. Let's not do this any more."

Tom surrendered the worms without a fuss and found something else to do.

That evening I thought about *anit. What do talking to animals and bathing earthworms have in common? Obviously, a thread of meaning ties them together into a single category, but what is it?*

Some time later, the matter became even more complicated. We were celebrating the June birthdays of Tom and Kathleen. My brother in America had sent us a Mr. Potato Head kit. Included were plastic eyes, noses, ears, legs, and arms to be stuck on potatoes to form funny little dolls. We had no potatoes, so we used onions. We made two little dolls and set them on the dinner table.

Two teenage Manobo girls, who helped Betty with household chores, came in from the creek with the laundry. When they saw the onion-head dolls, they screamed, *"Ed-anit heeyan!"* Without another word, they left for home and did not come back that afternoon. Usually, visitors came to our house off and on throughout the day, but that afternoon no one came. An eerie silence surrounded us.

We realized we were in serious trouble because we had promised not to break the *anit* taboo. We had not only broken the taboo again, but we had broken our promise. Our problem was that we didn't have a clue as to what *anit* was all about. I wondered, *How do these people know what kind of activity is considered* anit? *They had never seen a Mr. Potato Head kit before, yet they knew instinctively that it was* anit. *This is really strange!* Ironically, our Manobo friends seemed to feel that we were the ones who were really strange.

The following morning, I took a package of garden seeds for a gift and went to see Datu Ramon Lumansay, the most respected leader in the village. I climbed the ladder to his house. After a polite interval, I gave him the seeds and said, "Uncle, we did it again."

"That's right, you did it again."

"But Uncle, we don't have *anit* in America. How do you know what is *anit?*"

"We just know. How strange! I thought everyone in the world knew about *anit*."

"Uncle, if we are going to live here with you and study your language, it is important for us to know what kind of behavior can be *anit*. Please tell me everything you can think of that is *anit*."

He thought for a while. "You must not speak to an animal as if you were talking to a person."

"We know about that."

"Never give earthworms a bath."

"We know about that also. What else?"

"Don't put eyes, a nose, and ears on an onion."

"We won't do that anymore."

The datu sat back and began a story. "Years ago when I was a child, I heard about two young boys at a communal rice planting. With other boys and men, they were digging holes in the ground with their pointed dibble sticks. The women followed, dropping rice seed in the holes. Suddenly, a rat ran across the field. One of the boys shouted, 'There goes a wild pig. We must spear it!' They both chased the rat and speared it with their sticks. They were only playing, but what they did was *anit*.

"After the planting was finished that afternoon, a dark cloud appeared, and it began to rain. This was strange because rains were not expected for another week or two. The boys took shelter in a small field house nearby. A flash of lightning struck the shelter and killed them both. People said that Manewvanew was angered when they pretended a rat was a wild pig."

Datu Ramon continued, "It is also *anit* if a person marries a close relative. Marriage must not take place between a person and his or her parent, grandparent, or first cousin. A man must not marry his aunt or his niece. A woman must not marry an uncle or a nephew. We also consider this kind of behavior to be evil."

I began to understand why our friends believed that any seemingly minor infraction of the taboo was wicked and dangerous. In all societies around the world, breaking the incest taboos is considered among the most serious transgressions. I began to feel uneasy and knew we were in trouble. We might even be asked to leave! Talking to our cat apparently was as wicked as incest.

Datu Ramon cleared his throat. "It is also *anit* to sell a cat."

Now I was even more puzzled. We needed to know how to decide whether or not the Manobos might regard some ostensibly innocent behavior as *anit*. "Is there anything else we should know?" I asked.

"Yes," he said, "sometimes we break the taboo purposely. If we have conducted an unsuccessful hunt for a wild pig, we will find a leech in the forest and take it to the creek. We place it on a chip of wood and put it in the water. We say, 'Paddle, you rascal! You are floating away!' As a result, a strong wind will blow, a cloud will appear, lightning will flash, and rain will fall. Then the wild pigs will go into their burrows in the tall grass where they are easy to find and spear. If we are able to kill a pig, we offer it in sacrifice to Manewvanew, and the rain will stop. If we do not kill a pig, we offer a chicken instead. But we seldom do this because it is risky."

Datu Ramon could think of nothing more to tell me, so I expressed my thanks and went home. As I walked along, I thought, *We want to appear to be good people, but obviously our neighbors consider us and our children to be very wicked people.*

Cross-cultural missionaries always labor under a double burden. Personal integrity requires that they must be good persons according to the dictates of their own Christian consciences and culture. But the people they desire to reach must also see them as good persons. Often these two constraints draw missionaries in opposite directions and create frustration. For us the immediate need was to discover the semantic principle governing *anit*.

For the next few days, I puzzled over the list of taboo actions the datu had given:

- Do not talk to an animal as if you were talking to a person.
- Do not give earthworms a bath.
- Do not put eyes, nose, and ears on an onion.
- Do not pretend that a rat is a wild pig and chase it in a "just pretend" pig hunt.
- Do not marry a close relative.
- Do not sell a cat.
- Do not place a leech on a chip of wood and say to it, "Paddle, you rascal! You are floating away!"

We needed to make sense out of this and discover how to be "good" so we might effectively share our faith with our friends. *Dear Lord,* I prayed, *help us see what is so obvious to these people. We need to find the common thread of meaning that ties these different kinds of behavior together so they are considered to be the same thing.*

In retrospect, I can only say that the seed of an idea came from the Lord. I began to see commonalties in the list: First, only the behavior of a human could cause *anit*. An animal could not break the taboo.

Second, an action considered to be *anit* was always behavior toward a living thing—an animal, a vegetable, or a human.

Third, the infraction consisted of regarding a living thing as being something it was not. To state the taboo simply, it was a taboo against placing a living thing in an improper category. Cats, dogs, earthworms, and leeches are not human. Cats, dogs, and leeches do not have language. Earthworms do not take baths. Rats are not wild pigs; onions are not people. And probably most important of all, relatives are not nonrelatives. One can only marry nonrelatives.

The one restriction that did not seem to be explained by the pattern was, Don't sell a cat. This puzzled me for years until I asked Rosito, our translation assistant and a good source of information about the language. He had a semantic sixth sense. He explained, "It's very simple. If you sell a cat, it implies it is to be eaten. You may sell edible animals, but nobody sells a cat. A cat is not an edible animal. People can eat dogs, cows, and horses, but nobody eats cats."

My theory about *anit* seemed to work. We had no more problems deciding what might be improper behavior according to the taboo. Any theory, however, should be tested, but finding and implementing a proper test could be risky.

During our first furlough, a little boy provided us with a valid test. We were at a church in Santa Barbara, California, speaking to a Sunday-school class of first-grade children. We told about our lives with the Manobo people and our desire to win them for Christ.

After the class, a small boy approached us. "Do Manobo children have toys?"

"They have no toys like here in America, but the boys and girls do play with sticks, tin cans, or whatever they can find."

The boy nodded. "Tonight I am going to bring my favorite toy for you to take to the Manobo children." That evening before the service, he gave us a jack-in-the-box that was Popeye in a spinach can.

I smiled. "Thank you. We'll be sure to take it back to the Philippines with us."

That evening before we retired, I looked at Betty. "I feel certain this toy will be seen as *anit*. Perhaps this will be the test we need."

A few months later when we returned to the village, we took the jack-in-the-box with us. I got it out one afternoon when we had elderly visitors. I explained to the group that I didn't want to offend anyone, but we needed their opinion about something we had. The toy looked like a sardine can, so when I set it on the table in our living room, someone remarked, "Ah, sardinas." I pushed the button, and Popeye sprang out.

For a moment there was silence, then another person whispered, *"Ed-anit heeyan*! That will *anit*!"

The toy looked like a food can, but to the consternation of our visitors, the contents appeared to be human. Human beings are not food. They do not come in tin cans. It was easy to see why they whispered, "That will *anit*!" Their further reaction to the toy was interesting. It was almost as if it were pornographic. They were tempted to look at it but were trying hard to resist the temptation. I quickly closed it and put it away, and nothing more was said about it in our presence. We got rid of it at the next opportunity.

One anthropological tenet is that all rational human behavior is logical to those who understand the system behind the behavior. For us the seemingly illogical *anit* taboo became perfectly understandable once we discovered the simple logic that governed it. An effective cross-cultural missionary learns both language and culture. Learning a language that is unwritten is difficult, but linguistic tools enable a learner to write it down, look at it, and analyze it. Culture is more difficult. Behavior is not exactly culture; it is the manifestation of culture, of complex ideas hidden away in the mind, and these ideas are tricky to get at.

We are sure it was through God's grace and love for the Manobo people that we "stumbled" on the solution to the problem of *anit*.

# 8

# Help for a "Hot-Shot" Missionary

## 1955

One day, the director of our work in the Philippines, Dr. Richard Pittman, approached me. "Dick," he said, "I'd like you to find a spot among the Mamanwas where a couple of women translators can live and learn the language." He guided me to a map on his office wall and pointed to the largest southern island. "The Mamanwas are supposed to be in northeastern Mindanao, but they may be difficult to find."

"Why is that?" I asked.

"They're hunters, gatherers, and wanderers, and they don't stay in one area for long. So you may have to hunt for them."

"No problem," I said. As a young missionary linguist, I prided myself on my ability to travel easily and get along with people of other cultures. In the ensuing months, I searched the area twice but never did locate a suitable place for our team to live.

A year passed and again Dr. Pittman approached me. "Dick, I'd like you to have another look for those Mamanwas. I feel we should get someone settled among those people very soon."

"All right," I said. "I'll try again." I was confident that this time I could find just the right spot for my fellow translators.

A rural bus took me from the provincial capital to an area where a group of these illusive people supposedly were living. After several hours hiking up a rain-forested mountain, my guide and I approached the settlement but learned the Mamanwas had moved away. We returned to the road.

My disappointment soon turned to agony when I became ill with amoebic dysentery. Catching a bus to the city, I took a room in a small hotel with no air-conditioning in the tropical heat. I gulped down medicine and flopped on the bed. My third trip had failed, and now my quest looked hopeless. I tossed on the hard mattress with sweat running down my face and prayed, *Lord, what did I do wrong? Please help me.*

When I began to feel better, I opened my Bible and read, "Trust in the Lord with all thine heart; and lean not unto thine own understanding. In all thy ways acknowledge him, and he shall direct thy paths" (Prov. 3:5–6). Through those verses, the Lord showed me I had trusted myself instead of letting him guide me. I was my own reference point, so my role-playing was useless. Only he knew the proper place for two single women to live safely, learn the language, and translate and share God's Word. He might have even said to himself, "I'll allow Mr. 'Hot-Shot' Missionary to get a good case of dysentery and force him to set his sights on me." Now I prayed, *Lord, you have said, "Without me ye can do nothing"* (John 15:5). *I can't do this job without you. Please take over.*

After three miserable days of self-dosing, I finally felt well enough to continue my search. I made my way through the crowd at the bus station and found a seat on an ancient vehicle.

"Where are you going?" the conductor asked.

"I don't know," I said. "I'll tell you when I want to get off."

The bus rumbled over rough roads for a couple of hours. My thoughts were a jumble. *What am I doing? I haven't a clue where to get off. Lord, please show me.*

Finally, the bus crossed a beautiful river and stopped in a familiar village. When I had visited previously, a small settlement of Mamanwa people were living several kilometers upstream. The location seemed ideal then, but I remembered a warning from Mr. Salas, the local schoolteacher, about a nearby logging camp. "Single women wouldn't be safe," he had said. So why should I look here again? But a strong feeling came over me, and I seemed to hear a voice say within me, "Dick, get off the bus." *This is ridiculous,* I argued. *The Lord doesn't lead this way.*

The bus started forward, then pulled to a stop down the road. I seemed to hear the voice again, "Dick, get off the bus!" This time I obeyed. *Okay, Lord, I guess you know what you're doing.* I grabbed my bag, paid my fare, and climbed down.

Mr. Salas, who lived nearby, sat on his porch as I approached and greeted him. "Hello, Pare."[7]

He smiled. "You are here again, Pare?"

"Yes, I'm still looking for Mamanwas. Are they living upstream?"

"Yes, they are still there."

"How about the logging company? Are they also still upstream?"

He shook his head. "Oh, no, they've been gone almost six months."

I silently thanked God for his guidance.

A few weeks later, I accompanied two women missionaries, Doris McCorkle and Jean Shand, and helped them get settled in the village.

That was the beginning of over twenty-five years of ministry among the Mamanwas. These original missionaries later married and were replaced by two sisters, Jeanne and Helen Miller. They learned the language, taught the people to read, and finished translating the New Testament.

Today many Mamanwas trust the Savior. We received a letter from the Miller sisters, reporting that Julian, their first and most faithful translation assistant, went home to be with the Lord. He died singing scriptural songs he had composed with Manmanwa tunes.

I feel highly privileged to be part of God's sovereign plan for these people. It all began with a good case of dysentery for a "hot-shot" missionary who learned to trust God in everyday affairs.

---

7    *Pare* is a short form of *compadre*, meaning "fellow godfather."

# 9

# Meneminto

## 1957–60

A few months after Siblian came to faith in Jesus, Betty, our three children, and I were back in the village of Barandias. It was in June or July, so Siblian was working most of the time in his rice field.

We were preparing the final draft of the Gospel of Mark in Manobo for publication, and I often consulted Meneminto about some feature of grammar or the meaning of a word.

He was a man in his forties with a gentle spirit and a willing heart. But he was an invalid, suffering from a mysterious urinary ailment that caused bleeding if he did heavy work. As a result, he was always at home and available for my questions.

When I showed him our manuscript of Mark, he became interested, so I shared the gospel with him. One day as I was leaving his house, he asked me to leave the manuscript with him to read. Later that day, I returned and found him lying fast asleep, the half-read document covering his eyes.

It soon became obvious that through reading the Gospel of Mark, he had put his trust in Christ. "*Geli,*" he asked, "now that I believe in Jesus, how am I supposed to live and behave?" I encouraged him to trust God for guidance and to obey what he understood about God's Word.

Meneminto began to express his newfound faith by his actions, his joy, and his enthusiasm for Scripture. I started a Bible study of Mark with Siblian, Meneminto, and Rosito, the first three believers. We met on Sunday mornings under a tree near our house.

Some time later, I encouraged Meneminto to go with me to the Baptist clinic in Malaybalay to consult Dr. Lincoln Nelson about his ailment, but he seemed reluctant to go.

Finally, he asked, "Do I have to become a Baptist to be treated at the clinic?"

"No," I said, "Dr. Nelson treats anyone who comes to him for help. Patients are invited to receive Jesus as their Savior, but the decision to do so is theirs alone."

"How will I pay for treatment?" he asked. "I have no way to earn what it will cost."

"The payment will be small," I said. "But I will pay for you, and you can repay me when you are well enough to work again."

A week later, I accompanied Meneminto and his wife to the clinic. I was with him when Dr. Nelson examined him with a cystoscope. "Our brother has a large stone in his bladder," the doctor said. "This is what causes the bleeding and pain. Come back tomorrow morning, and we will remove the stone." He turned to me. "When he recovers, he should be as good as new."

The next day, we were back at the clinic. Linc invited me to "scrub" with the surgical staff and put on sterile rubber gloves. After all, I had assisted him several years before in a rain-forest surgery. This time I would be only an observer, but I knew that Linc wanted me there to give security and comfort to my friend and brother in Christ who had never been to a medical clinic before.

When the staff made Meneminto ready, we gathered around the surgical table as Linc committed the skill of his hands and the well being of his patient to the Lord. He administered an anesthetic, then went to work with two nurses assisting. A few minutes later, Linc used his forceps to plop the offending stone into my open palm before he closed up the site. The stone measured about an inch and three quarters in diameter and was rough and jagged. I took it home, washed it, and gave it to the patient.

Meneminto rapidly recovered. In a month or so, he was able to work again and to care for his family. He told me that the best part of his experience was when Dr. Linc prayed for him before the operation began.

Meneminto also grew rapidly in his walk with the Lord. One Sunday morning, he walked a mile down the hill from his field house to attend the chapel service. As he sat on a rough-hewn bench, he shook with chills and fever from malaria.

When I saw him, I asked, "*Geli*, why didn't you stay home today and have someone ask us for medicine?"

"I came," he said, "because I didn't want the Lord to think I don't love him."

Meneminto later became the treasurer for the infant Manobo church and was a faithful keeper of the Lord's money. He was also the treasury because he kept the accumulated money from offerings in a money belt around his waist. There was no nearby bank, and his bamboo-and-grass thatched house had no secure place in which to leave it.

One Sunday he rose to make an announcement. "This money that I carry around my waist is God's money," he said. "It is not your money, nor is it my money. I have never borrowed even five centavos of it, and neither will any of you!" Then he sat down.

Meneminto had a strong concern for his family and friends. One day he and I were walking in the village, and he said, "*Geli*, what about my dear old father? He never heard the gospel. Why didn't someone come to tell him?"

When I could answer, all I could say was, "*Geli*, I am so sorry. We came as soon as we could." Betty and I were just twenty-four-years old when we joined Wycliffe Bible Translators.

He and I often talked about the time when we would be together with Christ in heaven. "If Jesus is preparing a special place for Manobo people up there, I'd like to be with them," I told him. Meneminto, his wife, and many of our Manobo brothers and sisters are already there now, and I am a bit envious.

But I will never forget my gentle, faithful friend, Meneminto, who loved the Lord and loved his people.

# 10

# A Sick Boy

## 1956

One Sunday afternoon in the village at Barandias, our two-year-old, Tom, woke from his nap with a high fever and convulsions. Betty and I were frightened.

This was the rainy season, and the road was muddy and slick with deep holes and ruts. We had parked our Jeep at a friend's house five miles away. Even with four-wheel drive, we couldn't have driven the vehicle closer to our village. A bridge was out, and the Mulita River was too deep to drive through.

It would soon be dark—too late to leave for medical help at the clinic in Malaybalay, fifty miles (eighty-three kilometers) away. At this latitude, seven degrees north of the equator, the sun sets year around between 5:30 and 6:00 p.m., and darkness falls immediately.

We loved living with these people, even in this isolated village without modern conveniences, but now we felt vulnerable, frightened, and helpless. As we sat by Tom's bed, I prayed out loud, "Oh, Lord, help us get Tom to the clinic in time!"

That evening, we bathed our youngster in lukewarm water several times to bring the fever down. Then Betty held him in her arms while she sat in our rattan chair. A profound sense of God's peace and love overwhelmed us as we prayed and waited.

When Tom's fever subsided somewhat, we tucked him in bed and went to bed ourselves. Now all we could do was wait until morning to reach our Jeep.

When we awakened, Tom's fever was gone, but we still felt we should have the doctor check him. We left the house about 7:00 a.m. for the trek to our Jeep. Our friend Siblian carried Tom, and Anuy carried four-year-old Kathleen. She kept saying to Anuy in Manobo, "*Mezesen! Mezesen,*" which means "strong" or "hard." He thought she was commenting on his strong arms as he carried her Manobo style on his back, wrapped in a sheet. Since he had a thin, skeletal frame, I think she was referring to his bony back.

We got to our Jeep around 8:30 and piled in. By early afternoon before the rains began, we reached the gravel highway and turned northward toward Malaybalay. I drove while Betty held Tom in her arms. We prayed that our friend, Dr. Lincoln Nelson of the Bethel Baptist Clinic, would be home.

A few kilometers up the road, another Jeep approached us; the driver was Linc himself. We stopped him and explained that Tom had had a high fever and convulsions the day before. After a quick examination, the doctor found that Tom's temperature was rising again and diagnosed malaria. He wrote a note to his wife, a nurse, concerning Tom's treatment.

We thanked the doctor and continued toward Malaybalay. In another hour and a half, we were at the clinic where Lenore Nelson gave Tom a shot.

In a day or so, he was back to normal, and we gratefully returned to Barandias. Even though recurring attacks are common, Tom never had malaria again during his time in the Philippines.

This was another instance of God's constant care and the fact that our "steps" and our Jeep travels were "ordered by the Lord" (Psalm 37:23).

# 11

# A Promise Made

## 1957

In the early spring of 1957, I had a "holy urge," a strong desire to visit a neighboring tribal area where a group called the Matigsalug lived. Two of our colleagues, Norman Abrams and Gordon Svelmoe, had visited the area several years earlier and brought back intriguing reports. I suspected that the language of these people was closely related to that of our Manobo friends.

The Matigsalug people live in and near the Salug River Valley, which is on the eastern side of our province behind two mountain ranges. The name *Salug* is an old Philippine word meaning "the waters."[8] My Manobo friends in Barandias had a negative opinion of the Matigsalugs. "They're sorcerers," a Manobo told me one day. "Whenever anyone here is the victim of sorcery, we know it comes from the Matigsalug people."

When I heard that, my desire to visit them grew even stronger. I talked with one of the leading men in Barandias, Datu Eusebio Lantong. "Uncle," I said, "I want to go to Salug."

He frowned. "You don't want to go to Salug. There are bad people over there. It is too dangerous. They might kill you."

"I don't want to be killed, but perhaps you know someone respected by the Salug people who could guide us. Is there someone powerful enough to give us protection?"

---

8    R. David Paul Zorc, *Proto Philippine Finder List* (Ithaca, NY: Cornell University, 1971).

"Yes, I have a distant nephew, Datu Lorenzo Gawilan, who is the highest authority over all the people in the Salug Valley. He might go with you."

"Where can I find him?"

"He is often in the barrio of Dancagan, south of here. If he agrees to go with you, you will be safe anywhere in the area."

"Will you go with me to look for him?"

"I will."

My translation assistant, Siblian, was the stepson of Datu Lantong. He and his good friend Pidil agreed to accompany us. Since Pidil's father had come from the Salug area, he was curious to know more about his ancestors. An American missionary friend, Ron Esson of the Association of Baptists for World Evangelism, asked if he could join us. Another Manobo friend, Ugelinen, also decided to go along. We all rode in a passenger bus from our center at Nasuli to the town of Dangcagan.

When we reached the village, Datu Lorenzo Gawilan was not there, but his younger brother, Datu Ugtad Gawilan, offered to be our guide. "If you are with me," he said, "you will be safe."

Datu Lantong agreed that if we were in the care of Datu Ugtad, he would have no fears for us.

"How long will it take us to get there?" I asked.

Datu Ugtad seemed confident. "We can reach the Salug River in three days." But these strong, sinewy young men of the Mindanao rain forest did not realize how long it would take two American greenhorns to hike where they themselves could go with relative ease.

We slept that night in Dancagan. The next morning, we visited a local store to buy rice and dried fish—lightweight food that would keep well. Since this was the middle of the dry season, food would be scarce in interior villages until the rains returned in June. Our Manobo companions were delighted with our food supply, but we Americans soon found plain rice and dried fish difficult fare.

We started walking, and by midmorning of the first day, we reached the gorge of the Pulangi River, which we crossed on a precarious swinging vine bridge. We stopped that afternoon in Pontian, where Datu Ugtad lived, and the villagers warmly welcomed us. That evening we gathered in the local school where young people entertained us with beautiful folk dances to the exotic tinkling music of the *selurey* and the *kutiyapi*.[9]

The next morning, we moved south along the foot of the first mountain ridge. At noon we ate by a creek and bathed in a cool pool. Then we turned eastward again and plodded on a trail through tall *cogon* grass up Kianlud Mountain. With the sun on our backs, we became extremely hot and thirsty. Since Ron and I were the only ones carrying water and we shared it with the others, our canteens were soon empty.

Datu Ugtad had expected that by nightfall we would be over the mountain and into the village of Simud.[10] But by seven o'clock, we were only two-thirds of the way to the crest, and darkness had fallen. Ugtad announced we would camp on the mountainside near a spring. Ron and I flopped on the grass exhausted. The men steamed rice in green bamboo tubes and roasted dried fish in hot coals. Then we bedded down on wide banana leaves for sleeping mats and slept soundly.

In the morning, we ate the rest of the cooked rice and set out again with new energy. We soon reached the peak and moved quickly down the other side.

By noon we reached Simud, the first Salug village on our trip. It was a typical tribal village with evidence of squalor and obvious poverty, but the houses were neat and had flowers planted around them.

The people asked if we could help a woman who had been in labor since the day before. They were afraid she might die. Ron, a pharmacist at the Bethel Baptist Clinic in Malaybalay, often helped deliver babies, and he had brought along a simple medical kit. We started to the woman's home, but by the time we reached it, her child had already been born.

That night the people gathered to entertain us again with the music of the *selurey* and *kutiyapi*. To everyone's great delight, our companion Ugelinen reciprocated with a skillful and hilarious dance imitating a man robbing a wild bee's nest. Siblian accompanied him, beating two sticks on an empty five-gallon kerosene can.

---

9   The *selurey* is a harp made of bamboo. The *kutiyapi* is a boat lute (shaped like a boat). Both instruments are tuned to a pentatonic scale, which has five pitches per octave, in contrast to the seven-note heptatonic scale used in most Western music.

10   Today Simud or Sinuda, as it is now called, is a large town on the highway from Bukidnon Province to Davao City.

"Perhaps the Americans can offer some entertainment," a man suggested. "Surely, they know how to do something." Everyone looked expectantly at Ron and me.

I turned to Ron. "I learned an Irish jig in grade school. Do you think I should try it here?"

He grinned. "Go ahead."

I had danced only to an old fiddler's tune my father used to play, but the cadence that Siblian had beaten out for Ugelinen would be perfect. What followed was pandemonium with the laughing and shouting of the spectators, the deafening metallic banging on the kerosene can, and the clatter of my hiking boots on the bamboo floor. When I stopped, I had stomped my way into their hearts, and they shouted for more. After a few more passes around the floor, they seemed satisfied. I later realized I had set a precedent that would be hard to discontinue. Mysteriously, the news about my performance traveled ahead of us, so I had to repeat the performance in every village we visited.

Early the next morning, we set out again. We hiked for two days over two more mountains. Since there were few trails, we followed small creeks where the undergrowth was not so heavy.

It soon became obvious that the Matigsalug language was closely related to the Manobo that Betty and I were learning in Barandias.[11] The Salug people seemed to know what I was saying, but I had difficulty understanding much of what they said.

We finally descended into the Salug River Valley at a place called Tagawili. We were all worn out, and my boots were coming apart. Our trek to this point had taken us five days, far longer than any of us anticipated.

Siblian was badly frightened. He had never been so far from home nor so deep into what he considered unfriendly territory.

Because of the difficult terrain, Ron and I weren't looking forward to the trip back over the mountains. I had heard that the river was navigable by bamboo raft, so I thought if we could get the local people to make rafts

---

11    Matigsalug is one of about twenty languages of the Manobo subfamily of Philippine languages. In 1957 we did not yet have a clear picture of the relationships between the various languages of Mindanao. See Richard E. Elkins, "An Extended Proto-Manobo Word List," in *Panagani, Language Planning, Implementation, and Evaluation: Essays in Honor of Bonifacio P. Sibayanon on His Sixty-Seventh Birthday,* edited by Andrew B. Gonzales, FSC (Manila: Linguistic Society of the Philippines, 1984), 218-229.

for us, we could reach home without the difficult trek back across the two mountain ranges. With rafts, we could float down to the coastal highway and catch a bus back to our starting point.

Siblian balked at this. The trip by raft would take us even deeper into what his people called hostile territory. He thought we might be killed before we reached a safe area. Siblian and Pidil considered going back over the mountains by themselves, leaving the rest of us to take the river route. I felt responsible for Siblian, so said I would go with them. But Ron was not happy with this, and for a few minutes we seemed to be at an impasse.

At this point, our guide, Datu Ugtad, proved his leadership by taking the decision out of our hands. "We must not split up," he said, "as I cannot be responsible for the safety of anyone who leaves my care. If we stay together, we can travel the Salug River if we can secure rafts. If we can't get rafts, we will hike along the river downstream with no more mountain climbing."

Siblian and Pidil accepted this without further discussion.

News about who we were and what we wanted traveled quickly through the area. A datu upstream named Mampangendey sent firm word that no one was to make rafts for the Americans. If they needed anything, he said, they were to ask him for help.

I looked at my companions. "Brothers," I said, "here on the Salug River, it is as if we are no longer in the Philippines. We are beyond the authority and protection of the government. Evidently, this datu upstream is the law here, and I think we'd better do what he says."

Datu Ugtad nodded his approval, and we all agreed we should go upstream the next day.

In the morning, we ate a breakfast of rice and dried fish, then followed a trail up the river. Several hours later, we reached Panganan, where we had been told that Datu Mampangendey lived. It was not exactly a village, but in a flat area where the river made a wide bend, we found one large house situated on the bank of the river close to the foot of the hill. No one was around. We learned later that many people lived in the area but preferred to build their houses on the tops of ridges where they could see enemies coming, rather than on lower ground where they were vulnerable. The practice of *pangayew*, raiding and blood feuding, was still common.

In a few minutes, an elderly man and his wife appeared. The woman seemed somewhat demented, but we asked the man, "Grandfather, where is everybody?"

"They are up on the mountainside planting rice, but they will be back here this afternoon."

Following Ugtad's lead, we made ourselves at home. We ate lunch, bathed in the river, and washed our trail-soiled clothing.

Datu Mampangendey arrived with his people later that afternoon. Almost a hundred crowded into the house. We then witnessed an intriguing ceremony. The people, including small children, approached Datu Mampangendey and held out their right hands. With nods and smiles, the datu touched their fingertips with the fingertips of his right hand.

I looked at Ugtad. "What does that mean?"

"The datu is expressing his thanks for the labor of the people who helped him plant his rice field this morning."

Because Datu Ugtad was our guide and protector, we received a warm welcome. Everyone seemed to know him well, but they asked many questions about us two Americans and also about our Manobo companions from across the mountains.

Later that evening, I sat with Datu Mampangendey and his father, the elderly man we met when we first arrived. I had a standard word list of basic vocabulary in the Manobo spoken in Barandias, so I spent an hour eliciting the Matigsalug equivalents. This seemed to interest everyone in the house, and many sat nearby and helped answer my questions.

Then I opened my pack and pulled out the draft of the Gospel of Mark that Siblian and I had worked on. Siblian was not yet a believer nor were any of our friends in Barandias. Siblian had said to me months before, "You might get the young kids to believe these stories we are translating, but none of the old folks will ever believe them." Undaunted by his attitude, I wanted to take advantage of the opportunity that our visit here offered. Since the people seemed to understand our Manobo, I thought they might understand at least some of our translation. I wondered if they had ever heard anything about the gospel or the Bible.

I turned to Datu Mampangendey and his father, Mangulibey. "Grandfather, Uncle, have you ever heard of Jesus Christ?"

After a thoughtful pause, Datu Mampangendey said, "We have heard the name somewhere, but we have never met him. I don't think he has ever come here."

It was my turn to pause, and I prayed silently, *Lord, where do I begin?*

Immediately, the thought came, *Begin at the beginning.*

I looked at Mampangendey. "Uncle, long, long ago, the world was created."

"Oh, we know about that. It was *Manama* who created the world."

"Yes, and he created the mountains, the river, the deer, the wild pigs, and he also created the first two people."

"That's right," he said, "and we know their names, *Adan* and *Eba*, and they disobeyed because they ate the *mansano*."

The names *Adan* and *Eba*, Adam and Eve, obviously came from the Spanish, as did the word *mansano,* which comes from the Spanish word for "apple." I guessed that when the Spanish clergy came to the Philippines some four hundred years before, the creation story was passed along until it reached this valley, but not many, if any, of the New Testament stories ever reached this far.

I smiled. "Those first ancestors of ours, Adan and Eba, disobeyed, and we, like them, have also disobeyed."

The datu nodded. "That is true. I wonder why we always seem to do what is wrong and not what is right?"

"I have read in *Manama's* Book that one day he is going to punish the people in the world who have disobeyed him."

"We know about that, too, and it frightens us." He thought for a moment. "You know, you Americans live way out on the edge of the earth, and we Matigsalug people live right here in the center. When *Manama* comes to punish, he will get to you first. Will you come quickly here and tell us so we can get ready?"

I looked into his eyes. "That's the very reason why we came."

Fear leaped into his face. "You mean that *Manama* is right now on his way to punish us?"

"No, I have better news than that. *Manama* has a "big breath" (great love) for all people. So he sent someone special to rescue us so we will never be punished. His breath for us is so big that he sent his own Son to free us from being afraid of punishment. The name of his Son is Jesus Christ. We Americans have come here today to tell you about him."

I opened the manuscript of the Gospel of Mark and read, "This is the beginning of the good news about Jesus Christ, the Son of God."

Living with the Manobo people had taught us that the evil powers of the spirit world were real and active among them. Mark's Gospel speaks with great meaning to indigenous people because it includes more accounts of Jesus' power over evil spirits than any of the other Gospels.

For the next two hours, after emphasizing that Jesus Christ is much more powerful than any evil spirit, I went through the Gospel, reading about every occasion where Christ freed people from evil spirits.

Next, I read about Jesus' control over the weather as he rebuked the wind and storm and calmed the waters of a lake. This was significant because Manobo people believe that certain behavior angers the thunder god and causes people to be struck by lightning.

Then I read about Jesus' power to heal the sick and raise the dead. Manobo people believe that sickness is punishment for offending the spirits.

Finally, in my own words, I said, "Most important of all, Jesus is so powerful that he could take the place of every person who ever lived on earth and accept the punishment for every wrong act that anyone ever did. Because of his love for all people, he allowed himself to be killed by being nailed to a cross. His body was placed in a cave, and after three days, his Father *Manama* made him alive again. If we accept what he has done for us and invite him to be our datu, he will, by his good Spirit, always be with us and protect us. When we die, we will go to live with him forever. This is really good news. Since he took our punishment, he promised that if we follow him, *Manama* will never at any time, on this earth or after death, punish us for our wrong doings."

Eagerly listening, all the people in the house were crowded around me, and the two old men sat with me on the floor. My dear friend Ron was sitting on a nearby bench, weeping and praying.

What happened next will be forever stamped on my memory. I looked up at the elder of the two men, Datu Mangulibey. He took the Gospel of Mark manuscript out of my hand and held it in front of him. It didn't matter that it was upside down, since he couldn't read. He smiled with tears running down his face. He slowly turned the pages and gently stroked each page. Never before had I seen anyone lovingly caress the pages of Holy Scripture. It was only a typed manuscript, a bit crushed from my pack and not on India paper with gold edges and morocco bound, but to him it was sacred.

I closed my eyes and prayed silently, *Lord, if you never bless me again in any way, I will never complain. You have just given me a supreme blessing. I can now say with the apostle Paul that I have preached the gospel in a place where the name of Christ was not known before* (see Romans 15:20).

The next day, I overheard a conversation in which several people were discussing what I had said the night before. "Did you hear what the American was telling? How amazing it is! Can it really be true that *Manama* will forgive our sins?"

We spent several days in the village. On the last day, people from the whole area arrived and crowded into the house that night.

I looked at Datu Ugtad. "What's going on?"

"Mampangendey has called the datus from up and down the river to come for a meeting. They are going to decide whether or not the people in this valley should accept the Word of *Manama*."

While the elders parleyed at one end of the house, a young man played the *kudlung*[12] at the other end. A young woman played the *selurey* and danced gracefully.

I was sitting on a sleeping bench and eventually fell asleep. The exotic tinkling of the music and the rhythmic drumming of bare feet on the bamboo floor troubled my dreams. I had the feeling of being far, far away in a strangely different world.

Sometime in the night, Datu Ugtad shook me. "Wake up!"

It took me a while to realize where I was. "What is it?"

"The datus have decided that they and their people will accept the teaching from *Manama's* Word!"

The next morning we prepared to leave. Datu Mampangendey had arranged for three sturdy bamboo rafts to be built for us. He told us that his son and two nephews would guide the rafts down to where we could find transportation.

As we stood on the bank of the river, he turned to me. "Nephew, listen to me. I am now adopting you as my American son, but I want you to promise me something. Go get your wife and children and return here. We will build you a house. We will give you rice. You must come and live with us because I want my people to have *Manama's* Word."

I looked at him with conflicting feelings of joy and sorrow. "Uncle, I am sorry, but I cannot come now."

"Why not?"

"Uncle, we are translating *Manama's* Word for the people west of here beyond the Pulangi River. That is what *Manama* wants us to do first. But I promise you that when we have finished there and if *Manama* makes it possible, we will come and live here with you, and we will translate *Manama's* Word for your people."

---

12    A smaller version of the *kutiyapi* lute.

Just before we stepped onto the rafts, Mampangendey looked at Datu Ugtad, then at me. "If you had not come with this man, we would have killed you."

We set out from Panganan on three rafts and began our three-day trip lazily floating down the river. Ron and I were elated that we did not have to face the difficult six-day hike back over the mountains. The river was mostly calm that first day, but our guides told us we would have great fun in white water before long.

At the end of the day, we pulled our rafts out of the water onto a sandbank below a hill where a tiny house overlooked the river. Our raftsmen arranged for us to spend the night with the people there.

The next morning, we pushed the rafts into the river again, and I noticed how cheerful Siblian was. As we drifted along, he sang the *Ulegingen*,[13] a poetic epic of his people. I figured he had gotten over his fear of the water and the territory.

The rest of our trip was uneventful except when we entered the mouth of a boxlike canyon called the "Demon's Teeth" where the river turned to churning white water. We hung on tightly as with studied nonchalance and obvious skill, the young men guided the tossing rafts with long poles as we plunged over and around huge rocks. The raft I was on became jammed between two rocks and overturned. We weren't injured, but my pack and its contents were soaked. After a struggle to extract the raft and turn it right side up again, we continued.

On the afternoon of the third day on the river, we reached the town of Calinan where we caught a jeepney into Davao City and then a bus to the town of Digos. We spent the night there at the home of the Tentarellis, Baptist missionaries. We boarded another bus the next morning for Bukidnon and home. We left Datu Ugtad and Ugelingen in Dangcagan where they had joined us nearly two weeks before. While there, we were surprised to see Cliff Carlberg. He'd come to look for us because Ron's wife and the fellow missionaries in Malaybalay had become anxious. They had heard nothing from us since we left twelve days before. Siblian and Pidil returned to Barandias. All of us reached home that evening.

Several weeks later, Siblian came to our center at Nasuli, where Betty and I were staying, to tell us about something that had happened on our first night on the river.

---

13    Francisco Col-om Polenda, *"Ulegingen:* A Prose Retelling of a Mindanao Epic," translated and edited by Richard E. Elkins, *Kinaadman* XVI 2: 100–225, 1994.

I was badly frightened, not only by the fact that we were in alien territory but also because I could not swim. If our raft overturned in a rapid, I could easily drown. The creeks in our country are only a foot or two deep, but the Salug River is swift and deep in many places. Aside from the fears I felt for my safety, I was deeply disturbed because I had seen two elderly datus accept the message of the gospel. I was confused and realized I needed supernatural confirmation about what might be the truth. As I lay down to sleep, I offered a prayer to the gods of our ancestors, *If you gods are really who the old folks say you are, please let me know in a dream tonight.*

I went to sleep and subsequently dreamed. I saw a man standing at some distance with a book in his hand. With measured and deliberate steps, he walked toward me. As he drew near, he opened the book and held it out to me. I saw it was the Bible. The dream ended, and I woke up. As I thought about it, I realized it was not a god of my ancestors who had come to me. It was the true God, the Father of the Lord Jesus. I prayed again, this time to Jesus Christ, and I asked him to come and live in my life.

"*Geli,*" he said to me, "I am the only believer among our people, but even if I am the only one forever, I will never give up Jesus Christ."

He was, in fact, the first of a number of people in Barandias to trust in Christ. In the next few years, he shared his faith with many and several years later became the founder and first lay pastor of the church there.

In the ensuing years, Betty and I were busy in Barandias with the work of translation and all that it entailed. But my promise to Datu Mampangendey was never far from my thoughts. Would it ever be possible for me to fulfill that promise? I was sure that the long trek that ended in our meeting with him and his father was indeed the result of a holy urge. Would our sovereign Lord ever send Betty and me back there to live and work? We certainly hoped and prayed that this would be so . . . someday.

# 12

# God Sends Help for a Sick Child

## 1957

After the first trip into Matigsalug country, Betty and I returned to Manila to finish an assignment in the fall of 1957. Meanwhile in Barandias, Siblian's oldest child, Ben, became very ill, most likely with pneumonia.

Our Manobo friends seldom had any financial resources, but this was an especially difficult time. Siblian and his wife wanted medical assistance for their child, but they were destitute, and none of their friends or relations could help. They needed money for bus fare and doctor's fees but could borrow none. So they cared for their child as best they could as his illness progressed. Siblian, a new believer, prayed that God would somehow send help for Ben.

After a few days, nothing changed, so Siblian said to his wife, "I think we should go up to the field house. I feel so helpless. If we stay here, we can do nothing but sit and watch him become worse. There, at least, I can work in our rice field where hard labor can take my mind off our grief for the boy."

She agreed, and they wrapped the child up, loaded their water buffalo with supplies, and hiked to their hillside field.

A day or so later, Siblian woke up with the feeling that they should return to the village.

When he mentioned this to his wife, she said, "This is strange. Are you sure this is the right thing to do? We have been here only a short time, and now you want to go back? I am sure we'll have no more help for our child there than we have here."

"You're right," he answered, "but I have this strong feeling that we should return to the village. Perhaps God is sending us some help."

Reluctantly, she consented, and they returned to their house in the village. They had just arrived when they heard the sound of a jeep coming up the road.

When it stopped in front of their house, medical missionary Ron Esson got out. "I was passing by," he said to Siblian, "and I thought I would see how you're doing. I haven't seen you since our trip into Salug country."

"God has sent you!" exclaimed Siblian. "We have a very sick child, and we need your help."

Ron went back to the jeep for the medical kit he always carried when he traveled anywhere in the area. He quickly examined the boy and gave him an injection. He also gave the parents antibiotic tablets and other medicine with instructions for their use. Ron prayed for them and then drove away.

By the next morning, it was obvious that Ben was much better, and he quickly recovered.

When we returned to Barandias from Manila, Siblian told us how God had sent Ron to save Ben's life. "It is really true that we are big in God's breath," he said, using a local phrase for expressing the idea of love. "He does care for us always, especially when we can do nothing for ourselves. We can trust him."

# 13

# God's Field

## 1958

In late August of 1958, I had just returned to Mindanao from Manila with our four-year-old son, Tom, where an urologist told us that Tom had a congenital bladder obstruction. The specialist, the best urologist in the Philippines, said, "Your son needs surgery, and you cannot delay it for long, no more than three months. No one in this country can perform the surgery for such a young child. You must take him to the United States—and soon!"

Since it would take awhile to finalize travel arrangements, we returned to our home in Barandias among the Manobo people. We hoped that before we left, we could finish work on the Gospel of Mark and submit it for publication. This Gospel would be the first Scriptures available in the language of these people. We knew, however, that in order to finish, we would need the help of Siblian, our translation assistant, who was a new believer in Jesus.

When I asked him if he had time to work with me, he thought for a moment and said, "No, I don't think I can help. My rice field has been planted and weeded and is growing well, but I haven't finished putting up a fence around it. If it is not fenced soon before the rice matures, the deer and wild pigs will ruin the harvest."

"I understand," I said. "Your field represents a season's work, and it is the food supply for your family for the months ahead. Of course you must finish the fence."

Later, I said to Betty, "Siblian needs to work full time to complete the fence around his field. And that means that any further work on Mark will have to wait until we come back next year. But let's ask God to provide another way for us to finish it before we leave."

Soon Siblian and his family moved to their field house on the hillside where he worked on the fence. But a week later, we were surprised to hear the sound of activity around his house next door. I saw they had returned with kids, kettles, sleeping mats, and water buffalo. I approached Siblian. "Have you finished the fence?"

He shook his head. "No, I was not able to finish it."

"Then, why are you here? Is something wrong?"

"No, nothing is wrong."

"I don't understand."

He looked at me thoughtfully. "*Geli,*" he said, "each time I worked on the fence, all I could think about was the Gospel of Mark. I think God wants us to finish it before you leave."

"But what about your field?"

He paused for a few seconds and said, "I've given the field to the Lord. Now it's his field and his responsibility to do with it whatever he wants. Let's go to work and finish Mark."

As I walked back to our house, I was overjoyed and grateful to God. *It would be a wonderful testimony,* I thought, *if God would keep the deer and wild pigs out of the field so the fence would not be needed.*

That evening Betty and I prayed, "Lord, we need a miracle here. Please keep the field safe while we prepare your Word for these people."

During the next few weeks, we all worked diligently and finished the final details of the Gospel of Mark. Our director, Dr. Howard McKaughan, arranged to have a Bible Society consultant check it. The check was completed, and the manuscript was approved and accepted for publication.

On a Saturday morning as we were finalizing preparations to leave the village, Siblian was harvesting rice. We had prayed for a miracle, and I wanted to visit his field to see what God had done. So I hiked up to his hillside field. What I saw made me heartsick. The deer and pigs had destroyed the crop. For his season's work, Siblian had reaped only a sack and a half of unhusked rice, enough food for only a few weeks.

I walked over to Siblian and said, "*Geli,* I'm sorry."

"Why are you sorry?"

"Your field!"

He answered softly, "Not my field, *Geli*. God's field."

"But you and your family will be hungry this next year!"

He looked at me and said, "*Geli*, don't you have enough faith to believe that God will take care of us?"

I couldn't answer. The new convert was preaching to the missionary, and the missionary sorely needed the sermon.

"Listen to me, *Geli*," he continued, "Don't worry about us. We Manobo people know how to be hungry; we are often hungry. But remember this: it is far better for me and my family to be hungry for rice than for my people to be hungry any longer for God's Word."

I realized that a miracle had truly taken place. It was a miracle of the heart, a work of the Holy Spirit. Siblian's reasoning was in tune with eternity.

Betty and I and our three children left Barandias with full hearts and with trepidation about Tom's surgery. Betty had written to Vinnie and Marge Kretz, friends of ours in Seattle, Washington. Since Marge was a therapist, Betty asked if she knew of an urologist who might take Tom's case.

We were greatly encouraged by Marge's answer: "Vinnie's brother, Dr. Alex Kretz, is one of the best on the West Coast. He will take the case and won't charge you a cent." Marge scheduled an appointment for a few weeks later when we would arrive in Seattle.

Upon his examination of Tom, Dr. Kretz agreed with the Filipino doctor's diagnosis and subsequently performed the surgery. Time has shown that he did a masterful job, and Tom's recovery was without incident.

When we returned to the Philippines in January 1960, the printing of the Manobo Gospel of Mark was finished. We took copies with us when we returned to our linguistic center at Nasuli on Mindanao.

When our family physician, Dr. Lincoln Nelson of the Bethel Baptist Hospital, checked Tom, he remarked, "God must have a special task for this boy. The success of his surgery is nothing short of incredible."

After we had been home a few days, I went alone to Barandias to check on our house and let our friends know we were back. When we had left more than a year before, three people had believed in Jesus; now there were seven. Siblian and the other believers had shared their faith with members of their families.

I gave the copies of the Gospel of Mark to Siblian and asked, "*Geli*, what was it like while we were gone? Did you have enough to eat?"

"God provided for us in amazing ways," he said. "We had more food this past year than any other time I can remember."

Commitment is always a two-way street. When we become truly committed to God, he displays his commitment to us in wonderful ways. Faith had attained a strong foothold in Barandias. The little group of believers soon grew to thirty, and Siblian became the first lay pastor.

# 14

# Mempiyanu

## 1957–62

Some of the first people we met in Barandias were Catalino Libo and his wife. Catalino was the name he received at school. But everyone called him Mempiyanu, meaning "Father of Piyanu," their eldest child, and they called his wife Iney Piyanu, "Mother of Piyanu."[14]

When we first met him, Mempiyanu was barrio captain of Barandias. Philippine civil law required that each village or barrio have a council led by the barrio captain. In Barandias, this council was composed of men too young to have any say in village affairs. The older informal council of datus made the real decisions, but the younger men who had been to school were better prepared to understand and pass on requests from government officials.

A few months after we arrived, Mempiyanu and Iney Piyanu brought their very ill baby boy to us for treatment. We did what we could for the little one and gave him medicine. When he got better, his parents assumed he would recover and so did not return for more medicine. Unfortunately, he took a turn for the worse and died.

When we heard that the child was dead, Betty and I went to their house to offer what comfort we could. We went in and sat with them on a mat. The tiny body was lying in the center of the room, and Iney Piyanu

---

14   An adult parent is named *father* or *mother* of his or her oldest child. In Manobo society, the use of a real name is avoided to prevent a malicious spirit from using it to bring harm or misfortune to that person.

was crying. Betty put her arms around her, and I told them that there was a God who cared. We were still language learners in those days, but in a halting, awkward way, I tried to make the Good News about Jesus as plain as I could. I assured them that they could someday see their little one again.

As the years passed, I had repeated opportunities to share the story of Jesus with Mempiyanu. When Siblian and I began translating the Scriptures, I found that concentrated work was difficult in the front room of our house because a steady stream of visitors came and went during daylight hours. I hired Mempiyanu and Memputing to build a small study house in our backyard where I could translate with fewer distractions. While they were working, they became a captive audience who listened and made comments when I read them portions of the Gospel of Mark in their language.

One morning Mempiyanu came to borrow our hammer and saw. Tools were scarce in the community, and we were glad to lend ours, as they were a welcome addition to local resources. That evening at sunset, he returned the tools, and we sat on the porch and talked for a while. I felt led to ask him, "*Geli*," I said, "don't you think it is time that you and your family came to worship the true God with the believers in the chapel?"

He turned to me with a piercing look and said, "*Geli*, let me tell you something. It would be easy to be a Christian if you and Mother of Kathleen stayed in the village all the time."

"Why is that?" I asked.

"If you were here all the time, then when our children got sick, we could bring them to you, and you would give them medicine, and they would get well. But as it is, when a child gets sick, do you know what we have to do? We go to the *beyilan* (a spirit priest) and he, by divination, discovers which spirit is causing the sickness. He also determines what animal needs to be sacrificed in order to appease that spirit. Then we offer that sacrifice, and the child recovers. But if you were here all the time, we wouldn't have to sacrifice anymore. Being Christians would be much easier."

I thought for a moment, then turned to him. "Tell me, who do you think is greater, we with our medicine or Jesus Christ?"

"That's easy," he replied. "Jesus Christ is greater than you are."

"Well," I responded, "if you can trust us and our medicine when we are here, you can trust Jesus Christ when we are not here."

Mempiyanu thought about that for a few moments, then said quietly, "I am going now," and left for home.

He told me later that as he approached his house, his wife met him. "I think we are worshiping the wrong gods," she said.

"Why do you say that?"

"We are the most religious people in the barrio," she said. "We sacrifice often to the spirits at the graveyard, at the baliti tree, at the lake, and here in front of our house, but it doesn't do any good. We are the poorest of the poor, and our children are constantly sick. Our little girl, Melody, is sick again. We need to find a better god."

"Do you really believe that?" Mempiyanu asked.

"Yes, I do," she answered.

"Well, then," he said, "from now on, you and I and our children are going to join the others in the chapel on Sunday morning, and we will worship Jesus Christ."

The following Sunday, the believers and Betty and I were overjoyed to welcome Mempiyanu, Iney Piyanu, and their children to the little chapel. From that time on, they never missed a Sunday, and their growth in the Scriptures and in fellowship was evident. Life had improved for them and their family.

Some time later, God tested the faith of Mempiyanu and his wife. Betty and I were out of the village, and Melody again became ill. Mempiyanu told me later that they were sorely tempted to go to the *beyilan* and offer a sacrifice to save the life of their little girl. Instead, they asked the Christians to spend the night at their house praying for Melody. The child had not eaten nor drunk anything for three days, and all were sure that she was near death. As the night progressed, people took turns praying and singing hymns.

In the early morning hours, Mempiyanu took the sick child in his arms and prayed, "Lord, you know we love this little one, and we would like to keep her. But you love her too, and if you want her, you can have her." He began to weep and said, "Please, someone else pray."

While that person was praying, Melody stirred in his arms and said, "Daddy, I'm hungry. I want a drink of water." From that moment on, she quickly recovered.

Mempiyanu had passed the test, and the believers grew stronger in their faith. The truth of what I had said to Mempiyanu was affirmed, "If you can trust us and our medicine when we are here, you can trust Jesus Christ when we are not here."

Mempiyanu later became the lay pastor of the Manobo church and cared for his people with a true shepherd's heart.

# 15

# Announcements?

## 1962

Early in our second term in the Philippines, ten or fifteen adults in Barandias had come to faith in Jesus. We had not yet suggested formal church services to them because we felt the expression of this need should come from them. The believers themselves needed to take responsibility for the local church from the very beginning.

One day, Siblian[15] came to us and suggested that the believers in Barandias should begin to have church services.

I smiled. "Good idea!"

"You will be our pastor."

"No, I don't think I should be your pastor."

He seemed perplexed. "Well, who will be the pastor?"

"You will, and I will help you prepare your messages."

He thought for a moment, then asked, "How should we have church services?"

Here Betty and I needed to be careful. We did not want to impose on this Manobo community the forms of a foreign church that they might regard as sacred or even magical. The religious heritage of these people was shamanistic animism, which is the belief in and the manipulation of the spirit world. A main concern of any animistic religion is making certain the rituals and magic formulas are letter-perfect. We did not want

---

15   Siblian's formal name was Francisco Col-om Polenda

the church services to become a ritualistic way to manipulate God like the local shaman's rituals were intended to manipulate the spirits.

In any cultural setting, the worship of the church should fit the particular forms, needs, and abilities of the local society. It should also be meaningful in terms of their language and culture. In any valid worship anywhere in the world, meaning should be king, and form should be its servant.

I looked at Siblian. "How would you like to have church services?"

"We need to pray."

"Good idea."

"We need to sing Christian songs."

"Good idea."

"And someone should teach."

I smiled. "Another good idea. We'll leave it to you to plan the meetings, and I will help you prepare the teaching." I did not offer any suggestions as to the order of service.

The men of the infant church immediately began a building program. They cut small logs in the local forest and prepared bundles of *cogon* grass for roofing the chapel. Betty and I provided the nails. The building was small, about twelve by fifteen feet, with split-board walls and benches of rough-hewn boards supported by short posts set into the dirt floor.

In the weeks that followed, I met with Siblian on Saturdays to help him work out what he was going to teach. I left the selection of passages to him. He used the Gospel of Mark in Manobo and the Cebuano Bible in the local trade language.

Our Manobo friends were not fluent speakers of Cebuano, but they understood simple expressions, and they had no alternative. It would be years before they would have a complete Manobo New Testament.

Siblian was naturally literary,[16] and he did well at his preaching and teaching from the beginning. After we had worked together for a few Saturdays, he said, "I think I can do this by myself from now on."

---

16    Twenty-nine years later, Siblian became well known in the Philippines as the author of a volume of essays, *A Voice from the Hills: Essays on the Culture and Worldview of the Western Bukidnon Manobo People,* translated and edited by Richard E. Elkins (Manila: Linguistic Society of the Philippines; Summer Institute of Linguistics, 2002). Siblian wrote the book in Manobo, and Betty and I translated it into English. For this work, he was awarded a National Book Award for the best book of essays written in 1989. In 1994, his long article, *"Ulegingen:* A Prose Retelling of a Mindanao Epic," was also published.

With that, Betty and I became spectators on the sidelines as the church grew in spirit and numbers. We did work with Siblian and others to prepare a hymnbook, but for many years, our focus was on Bible translation and literacy. In a sense, we were leaders, but we stayed in the background and gave sparing advice only when asked.

It wasn't long before the church grew to about thirty members. The men sat on one side, and the women on the other. A few years later, the office of lay pastor shifted to Mempiyanu when Siblian became barrio captain.

The men of the church developed their own twist on Sunday school and took turns teaching. At the end of each lesson, the teacher would appoint another man to teach the next Sunday. In this way, every man had an opportunity to teach. We were often blessed when, under the guidance of the Holy Spirit, the Sunday-school lesson and the pastor's message challenged the believers in similar ways. Years later when the entire New Testament was published, qualified teachers were ready to take responsibility for witnessing and distributing the Scriptures wherever Manobo was spoken.

When the church held business meetings after the services, Betty and I left. We wanted them to know that decisions were their responsibility and should not be influenced by us. Leaders sometimes came to us with questions, but we referred them to the Scriptures and then let them make their own decisions.

Betty and I were occasionally away from Barandias, since I was involved in the translation checking and consulting program for other Wycliffe members in the Philippines. One day during our third term, we returned to the village. Rosito, our translation assistant, came to us, and we could see he was upset. "You knew the right way," he said, "but you never told us!"

I was puzzled. "What do you mean?"

He explained that a certain Filipino pastor had come to the service the previous Sunday. "At the end, the pastor said, 'It is obvious you people don't know how to worship God!' He gave us a paper where he had written the proper order of service. Why didn't you tell us? We were greatly humiliated by what he said." Rosito had been selected to come to us because he led the worship service.

I thought for a moment. "*Geli* Rosito, you must believe me when I say God requires no particular way for worship. Virtually nothing is written in the New Testament about it. No one, I mean no one, has the right to tell you Manobo people how to order your services. Even Betty and I do not have that right. We never said you must worship in any particular way because ways of worshiping God differ all over the world. Believers must be allowed to worship in ways that fit their particular culture. You are perfectly free to choose any way you like to have your services and to worship in ways that are comfortable for you. That pastor is a good man, but perhaps he doesn't understand that a people's culture and particular needs should determine how they worship."

I looked at what the pastor had written. He was a city-trained preacher and was used to the forms of worship in big-city churches that were like typical churches in the West. The list began with the doxology, followed by an opening prayer, a prayer hymn, and the pastoral prayer. Then another hymn was followed by announcements. Special music and another hymn came before the pastor's message. After the sermon, there was an invitation hymn, the invitation, and the pastor's closing prayer.

I turned to Rosito. "The way you have been conducting the worship service is fine, but you are always free to change it any way you like. The visiting pastor loves the Manobo people, and he wants to be helpful. I suggest that out of respect for him, Mempiyanu should call a meeting of the church leaders and consider his list. If anything on it seems beneficial, adopt it. If you feel that nothing should be changed, continue what you have been doing."

As Rosito left, I said to Betty, "Announcements! That's ridiculous! Why would they want that? In a small face-to-face society like this one, what would they announce? Pastor Mempiyanu would stand up and say, 'Next Sunday when the sun is about halfway to the top of the sky, we will begin our service. If we know you are coming, we will wait for you. We will begin with Sunday school and then have the worship service. After the service, we will go home.' But everyone knows that anyway. Everyone always knows what is going on except us—the Americans—and we never seem to know what's going on."

The next Sunday morning as Betty and I hiked down to the village, we wondered if anything would be different. We entered the chapel and sat down. In a short while, Rosito began the service by leading a few hymns. *That's a blessing,* I thought. *No change.*

But then Mempiyanu stood up and said, "This morning we are going to do something different; we are going to have announcements." I groaned inwardly as he continued, "Does anyone have anything they would like to announce?"

What happened next was a blessed surprise. A woman stood and said, "I want everyone to praise God with us. Since we have believed in Jesus, our lives have been changed, and we are so thankful!"

Then a young man stood and said, "Brothers and sisters, pray for me and help me. I have been telling my cousins over on the next hill about Jesus, but they don't want to believe. I must be doing something wrong, and I need your help."

A man said, "Pray for my children; they are sick with dysentery."

Another man confessed, "I have offended one of you here, and I want to ask for forgiveness. Please forgive me, and pray that I will learn to do what is right."

I was stunned. I bowed my head and prayed silently, *Lord, thank you so much that you did not allow me to open my big mouth and say to Rosito, "The church certainly doesn't need announcements."*

Rosito was busy at the makeshift blackboard making notes about all that had been shared. When there were no more announcements, he led the group in meaningful prayer and praise for all the concerns.

As Betty and I hiked home after the service, I thought about the announcements. The group had adopted the label for a necessary form in our Western church contexts, but they had interpreted it in terms of their own cultural needs. Actually, it was the very thing missing in the Manobo church, and it became a regular part of their services. I was sure the Lord was pleased with the believers' "announcements." We were all blessed and drawn closer together.

# 16

# Faith-Promise Giving

## 1963

It was Sunday morning, and members of the Barandias church had gathered for their regular service. Just as the service began, a pastor from a nearby town arrived and asked for permission to speak. He told the assembled believers they should be involved in faith-promise giving to support Filipino missionaries. "Each of you should promise to give a certain amount during the next year," he said. "Then you can trust God to supply the money necessary to fulfill that promise. A church your size should give at least two hundred pesos."

While the puzzled members watched, the visiting pastor held up a large chart that looked like a thermometer and indicated the two-hundred peso mark. Then he handed slips of paper to the people and said, "Just write down the amount of your promise so you won't forget."

This procedure caused considerable bewilderment among our Manobo brothers and sisters. They had assigned the office of treasurer to Meneminto, who kept the church funds in a money belt constantly around his waist. This was necessary because the village had no bank and no way to keep money safely in a house. The amount he cared for was never very much.

Offerings were minuscule by Western standards, usually no more than a few pesos a Sunday, but the needs of the congregation were also minimal. No Sunday-school materials were available in their language, the pastor received no salary, and materials for repairs or improvements of the building were available in the nearby rain forest.

When the need arose, the members contributed their labor freely, but they had little need for monetary offerings. In the past, they had been tribal people who practiced subsistence farming, and money was not important. We knew from our dealings with them that none of them ever had much of it. I suspected that most members wrote amounts on the slips largely because they did not want to commit the unthinkable offense of bringing shame to themselves or their church.

When the visiting pastor collected the promise slips, the total amount was seventy pesos, a little more than seventeen dollars in American currency. He was visibly disappointed but left without much comment.

I accompanied him down the path to the road where he waited for a bus. "Brother, don't be discouraged," I said. "Because of your concern for them, these Manobo believers have taken a significant step forward. We have never emphasized giving before because there was not much need for it. But now you have challenged them to consider the needs of lost people in other places. Let us wait and see what God will do through this." I stayed with him until a bus arrived, and he left.

When I returned to the chapel, the believers were standing outside around the pastor and other leaders. They were having a spirited discussion about what had taken place, and they obviously were not happy.

The pastor, Mempiyanu, said to the group, "You cannot ignore these promises you made this morning. You must give what you wrote down." He turned to the treasurer, Meneminto, and asked, "*Geli*, how much money does that belt around your waist contain?"

Meneminto removed the belt and carefully counted the money. "We have a little more than two hundred pesos."

Mempiyanu continued, "Very well, then, give *Geli* MengKaklin ("Father of Kathleen") seventy pesos to take to Malaybalay to pay the amount our congregation has promised. We don't want to bring shame on ourselves and our church if our people do not give what they have promised." He turned to the members. "This doesn't mean you do not have to give what you promised. It just means that we will not be shamed if you don't give."

Betty and I were away from the village a few weeks later when a young Bukidnon pastor and his wife asked if they could share with the church their plans to go to the Tigwa Manobo people as missionaries.

The members gladly agreed to this. They considered this pastor to be "their kind of person." The Bukidnon people speak a language that is closely related to the Manobo spoken in Barandias.

When the pastor and his wife came, they told the group how God had called them to the Tigwa people. They said they were trusting God to supply their needs. After they left, the church decided they would help support this couple by giving them ten pesos a month.

Some time later, a young lowland Filipino woman came to tell the church about her call to be a missionary in Thailand. The members welcomed her, and after she had spoken, they promised her also that they would give her ten pesos a month.

By this time, the promised giving by the Manobo church for the year totaled three hundred and ten pesos. When the year ended, the church had given more than one thousand pesos to missions. We did not know nor could we imagine where the money came from, but God supplied abundantly what they promised to give.

The result of all this was that the fledgling Manobo church learned how to give. They also learned that God blesses a church that participates gladly in fulfilling the Great Commission, for the congregation grew significantly that year.

Today at least four people from Barandias are in full-time ministry somewhere in the Philippines.

# 17

# Wild Ants?

## 1963

Dr. Eugene Nida, former translations secretary of the United Bible Societies, says that no word in one language has an exact equivalent in any other language. This seems a rather rash generality, but after working with many languages over the years, I have never found an exception to it.

A productive way to find out what a word means is to ask proper questions. Those that call for yes or no answers are not helpful because they only make a person guess one way or the other. Questions that begin with *what, where, who, when, how,* and *why* are productive. They require persons to think and give answers based on what they know or do not know about their languages.

I was once checking the Gospel of Mark in an indigenous language of eastern Mindanao. The translators were two single women and their translation assistant. At the translation center at Nasuli, we sat around a table with commentaries and various Bible versions spread before us.

Using feedback on the text, checkers ask questions of native speakers. I worked with a "back translation," a literal rendering of the translated text into English. Such a translation should use good English grammar but be semantically literal.

We were considering Mark 1:13: "And he [Jesus] was in the desert forty days, being tempted by Satan. He was with the wild animals, and angels attended him" (NIV).

The vernacular back translation read, "Wild animals were his companions." Since it is ambiguous in English, the term for *wild* is often a problem. It can mean wild in the sense of an untamed animal, or it can be a dangerous animal, which is what the Greek word *therion* means. The Philippine rain forests contain many wild animals, such as deer, monkeys, and squirrels but few really dangerous creatures.

So I said to the two American translators, "Ask your translation assistant to list all the wild creatures he can think of."

The assistant responded with a big grin. "I can do better than that; I'll go get one." He was down the steps of the house in a flash. The two women looked at each other and groaned. Their chagrin was even greater when he returned with a tiny, biting ant in his fingers.

"Wait!" I said. "Ask him what else. I want him to name everything else he can think of that can be wild."

So in his language he began, "Ant, hornet, wild boar, scorpion, wild dog, wild water buffalo, cobra and other poisonous snakes, and a large python. That's all I can think of."

I asked him the clincher: "Why do you say these creatures are wild?"

"Because they all can hurt you, and some can even kill you."

The expression meaning "wild animal" in Greek and this language did not match exactly, but they shared the basic component: harmful to humans. Even a tiny biting ant was wild in that sense for these people. Because this meaning component was in focus in the biblical text, I declared that the rendering was a good translation.

Translators are made, not born. They learn by experience how to ask good questions. These particular translators had carefully chosen the correct term, but they had a bad moment when their assistant came back with an ant as an equivalent for *wild animal*.

Bible translators soon become accustomed to surprises.

Betty and Dick Elkins with Tom, Dan, and Kathleen
(1960, left to right)

Dick, Betty, Kathleen, and Tom on the front porch of their first
house in Barandias (1955)

A moveable two-tiered shelf holds commentaries and study helps
while Dick works on translation projects.

Dick Elkins, co-translator Siblian, and Siblian's daughter, Edie,
with the first printed copy of the Manobo Gospel of Mark (1960)

The first chapel in Barandias (1961)

The JAARS plane arrives at Pangi near Barandias with the first
copies of the Manobo New Testament (1978).

Dick gives a Manobo New Testament to Pastor
Saturnino Linog (1978).

The Matigsalug datu, Mampangendey, his wives,
and children (1957)

Dick reads the Manobo Gospel of John to
Matigsalug people (1964).

Betty shows family pictures to Matigsalug friends (1987).

# 18

# A Well-Worn Envelope

## 1964

In the fall of 1964, Pastor Forrest Johnson of Tabernacle Baptist Church in Seattle, Washington, and his wife, Mary, came to the Philippines to visit Baptist missionaries. They graciously included us in their itinerary. Pastor Forrest had a heart for God and for missions. Betty had grown up in that church, and I had become a church member also following our wedding.

Our Jungle Aviation and Radio Service (JAARS) pilot flew the Johnsons to our village, and they stayed overnight with us in our bamboo-and-thatch cottage.

The next morning Siblian came to me and said, "We should have a special service and ask Pastor Johnson to speak. You can interpret for him." Pastor Forrest agreed, and in a short time the believers gathered to hear him.

The miniscule thatched chapel measured about twelve feet wide and fifteen feet long. Rough-hewn planks set on posts in the dirt floor furnished the seating. The thirty people gathered had a strong sense of togetherness. Desperately poor and poorly dressed, these believers displayed a nobility far beyond anything that affluence or prestige could offer.

When Pastor Forrest finished his relevant and powerful message, some listeners were in tears.

Then Siblian stood up and spoke in Manobo to the congregation. "At this time," he said, "we are going to receive a love offering for our dear brother, Pastor Johnson, and his wife." Forrest and Mary did not understand anything he said, and we chose not to enlighten them.

Someone passed a straw hat up and down the crowded benches. In a moment or two, Siblian left the chapel with the offering and soon returned with it in a well-worn envelope. He asked Forrest and me to come and stand at the front. Siblian handed me the envelope and asked me to present it to Forrest.

"Pastor Johnson," I said, "this is a love offering for you and Mary from these dear friends and fellow believers."

For a moment, Forrest stood in shock, and his face turned pale. "I cannot accept this, Dick," he whispered, "not from these poor folk."

"You have to accept it, Forrest," I said. "They are saying thank you for the gospel. You and the saints at Tabernacle Baptist made it possible for us to come. These folks will probably never have more than a tiny share of this world's goods, but they are now enriched with a wealth and a dignity that is beyond our wildest dreams."

Forrest turned to Siblian, took his hand, and struggled to keep his composure as he offered his thanks. An hour or so later, he and Mary left to resume their visit to other mission stations.

When this happened, Betty and I were in the process of packing up to leave for our second furlough in the United States.

A few weeks later, we were in Seattle. One Sunday after church, Pastor Forrest and Mary invited our family to their home for dinner. Several deacons of the church joined us. After the meal, Forrest handed me the envelope that still contained the bills of Philippine currency and asked, "Dick, how much is this in American money?"

I opened the envelope and counted the offering. "This amounts to three dollars and sixty-eight cents."

"I am buying this," he said. He opened his wallet and gave me the exact amount. "You may use this in any way you like for the Lord's work."

I handed him back the money. "This is for Camp Gilead," I said, referring to the camp Pastor Forrest had started in Carnation, Washington, in the 1940s. "When I was young, God called me to be a missionary at a Bible camp. Perhaps he will use this to call other young believers to take the Good News to a people who are still waiting."

Forrest kept that envelope with its Philippine pesos as a sacred memorial of the power of the gospel.

A number of years later, Betty and I saw it again. Forrest had "gone home" to heaven. We were visiting Mary, and she showed it to us.

Thinking back, I realize that most of the people who were in the little chapel are now with the Lord. I am sure that some day Jesus, who multiplied five loaves and two fishes, will tell us what he has done at Camp Gilead with those few Philippine pesos in that well-worn envelope.

# 19

# The Sovereignty of God and Knots in a Rattan Calendar

## 1964

Our Matigsalug and Manobo friends were seldom precise about the timing of an event, for few had clocks, watches, or printed calendars. In the daytime, the sun's position was their clock. If they wakened in the night, they could tell if dawn was near by the stars' positions.

The Manobo Christians always met on Sunday morning for services, but the time varied from week to week by as much as an hour or two. When the sky was overcast and they couldn't see the sun, the services would be later than usual.

For this reason, our friends were more event-oriented than time-oriented. Carrying out an event properly seemed more important than starting at a particular hour. They were, however, more precise about making sure an event took place on a particular day.

In 1964, eighteen years before Betty and I lived among the Matigsalugs, our JAARS pilot, Bob Griffin, flew me to the village of Panganan for a few hours' visit. We flew in a Heliocourier, a plane that could land and take off on a short strip.

I had arranged to have this new and rather rough airstrip built some months prior when fellow translator, Dan Weaver, our co-translator, Rosito Lumansay, and I had stopped there on a trek through that country. We had traveled for five days to reach Panganan then, but now with the airstrip, we could reach it in twenty minutes.

After a short visit, the headman, Datu Mampangendey, asked me, "When will you be back?"

"I'm not sure," I said. "I hope to visit again in about six weeks."

We climbed into the plane and took off. The strip was only 270 yards long, but with a light load in the Heliocourier, we were airborne with fifty yards of strip to spare.

After returning to our home in Barandias among the Manobos for six weeks, Betty and I went to our translation center at Nasuli to prepare for our second furlough in the States.

One morning, I walked up to the hangar and approached the pilot. "Bob, can you fly me in to Panganan for a last visit before we leave the country?"

He shook his head. "The schedule for this week is absolutely full. If there's a cancellation, I'll let you know. But you'll have to be ready at a moment's notice."

I assumed the flight would not happen, so I put it out of my thoughts.

But at ten o'clock two days later, Bob roared up to our house on his motor scooter and shouted, "Dick, let's go to Panganan!"

I grabbed a few things as gifts for Datu Mampangendey and ran to the hangar where Bob was getting the plane ready to go. In a few minutes, we were airborne for the short flight over the mountains and down the Salug River Valley to Panganan.

Since the village is in a deep, narrow valley with hills on both ends of the airstrip, landing takes much skill. Just as we were about to touch down, a horse ran across the strip in front of us. Bob hit full power and climbed steeply to get us high enough to come around again.

When we finally touched down, people were lined up on either side of the runway dressed in their special-occasion finery of beads and embroidered clothing. We climbed out, and they greeted us enthusiastically as they crowded around the plane.

As I shook Datu Mampangendey's hand, I asked, "What's the occasion? Why is everyone all dressed up?"

He grinned. "We were expecting you today."

"But how did you know we were coming?"

"We cut the last knot off our rattan calendar this morning, and by that we knew you would be here today," he explained. "You told me you would be back in six weeks."

Then I realized that we had been there exactly forty-two days before.

The Matigsalug people have a calendar that allows them to keep track of the days until a future planned event. It consists of knots tied in a strip of split rattan, one knot for each day. When I previously told the datu I would be returning in about six weeks, he made a calendar of forty-two knots, one for each day of the intervening time. Each day he cut off one knot.

The people gathered around us on the airstrip, so I shared the gospel and read from the Gospel of John in Manobo.

While we flew back to the center, I reflected that Datu Mampangendey was not the only one who had a calendar that determined the day of our arrival. Our sovereign God also had a calendar, and he had orchestrated our flight on that particular day.

"The steps of a good man are ordered by the Lord: and he delighteth in his way" (Psalm 37:23). I cannot claim goodness on my own, but with great joy I claim the righteousness of Christ imputed to me.

On this basis, I know that a loving Lord orders my steps—and flights.

# 20

# God's Guitar

## 1974

While living in Manila during our son Dan's final semester of high school, I felt urged to buy a guitar and take lessons. I argued with myself about it, saying that learning to play a guitar was for young people and not for a man crowding fifty. But the idea was persistent and wouldn't go away. Finally, one Saturday, I said to Betty, "I'm going to buy a guitar."

Together Dan and I made the rounds of several music stores where guitars were sold, but I was not satisfied with any instrument I saw. "Maybe we should try one more store that I know about," I said. "An instrument there may be more expensive, but it could be what I'm looking for." As it turned out, I did find a nice instrument at a reasonable price. While paying for it, I asked the clerk, "Do you know where I can find a teacher?"

"We teach guitar right here," he answered, "but we only teach classical guitar."

I grinned. "That's exactly what I want."

"Leave me your name, address, and phone number," he said, "and I'll have one of our teachers call you." A few days later, the teacher called and made arrangements for me to begin lessons.

My teacher was a talented young college graduate whom everyone called "Butch." I began weekly lessons and practiced in my spare time.

One day Butch told me he would be out of town for a few weeks on what he called a "lay apostolate." He and another guitarist planned to travel in the central Philippines, playing in churches, jails, convents, and orphanages.

When Butch returned, he called me, and I went to the store for a lesson.

Afterward, he told me about his trip. "We were on the Island of Siquijor," he said, "which is famous for its witches." He paused and then asked, "Dick, do you believe in witchcraft?"

I nodded. "I surely do."

Butch was surprised. "Really? I thought Americans didn't believe in it."

"Butch," I said, "I don't practice witchcraft or have anything to do with it, but I believe the devil, Satan, gives some people power to do strange, even miraculous things. We Christians, however, have no reason to fear witchcraft or any evil power, not even Satan himself. Christ, the righteous Creator of everything, lives in us and is with us, and he has defeated Satan."

Butch looked at me with wide eyes. "For many years, I've been haunted by evil spirits," he said. "They often come into my room at night, and I'm very frightened. Objects on the table move about seemingly by themselves."

"What have you done about it?" I asked.

"I went to a priest," he said, "and he didn't know what to do. But my mother knows a nun, and she gave me a Bible, a crucifix, and a rosary. When I read the Bible and pray the rosary, the spirits leave me alone. That rosary is really powerful, isn't it, Dick?"

I thought for a moment, then I said, "The rosary and crucifix are *symbols* of faith, Butch, but the Bible is the *substance* of our faith. 'The word of God is quick, and powerful, and sharper than any twoedged sword' (Hebrews 4:12). The Bible's truth is what the evil spirits can't stand."

Then I told Butch about an experience I had years before when I was in the Manobo village where we later lived and worked on Bible translation. I was in a friend's house trying to sleep when suddenly, the bamboo floor underneath my mat began to shake. Since I was still young and a newcomer to the Philippines, I had never thought much about evil spirits except in a theological way. I was in a small room by myself, and the only other people in the tiny thatched house were two other Americans who were sound asleep and unaware of what was going on. Siblian, who owned the house, had moved in with his stepfather and had left the house to us, his guests. I was not afraid, but I was extremely puzzled.

I made several trips outside in the dark with my flashlight to see if there was any reason for the shaking. I thought a local joker might be playing tricks on us, but I learned later that Manobo people don't joke about the supernatural. "If you joke about the spirits," one said, "they will come around to see what you're doing." I also thought a water buffalo might be scratching his back against one of the house posts, but a fence was around the house, and no animal could enter the yard. I discovered no ordinary reason for the shaking, which began every time I lay down.

After some time, it dawned on me that the cause might be supernatural. Then a verse popped into my mind: "Ye are of God, little children, and have overcome them: because greater is he that is in you, than he that is in the world" (1 John 4:4). Sitting there on my trembling sleeping mat, I prayed silently, *Lord, I think this is not my problem; it is your problem. If this is something evil, I place it in your hands.* Immediately, the shaking stopped. I lay down and went to sleep.

After I finished the story, I looked at Butch. "If we ask Jesus Christ to live in us and take care of us, he will do it," I said. "Because he is in us, the spirits are afraid of us because they are afraid of him (see Mark 5:7). But we have to ask him to be part of our lives." I paused. "What kind of Bible do you have?"

"It's a Gideon Bible."

"I think you need a Bible in your own language, Tagalog, or perhaps one in modern English that would be easier to understand."

"I'd rather have an English Bible," he responded. "Where can I get one?"

"I'll bring you one."

"Oh no, just tell me where I can buy one." So I told him that on United Nations Avenue, either the Philippine Bible House or the Overseas Missionary Fellowship bookstore next door would have what he wanted.

"I go right by there on my way home," he said. He literally ran out of the store and left me standing there.

When I reached home, Betty and I prayed for Butch.

The next evening during supper, he called me. "Thank you for talking to me, Dick," he said. "I got saved!"

The following week after my lesson, Butch told me what happened: "I went to both stores, and I couldn't find the kind of Bible you mentioned. But I did find another book by Theodore Epp called, *How to Resist Satan.* I read it twice, Dick, and it was very meaningful to me. The next morning, I got up early and went to the church in Plaza Santa Cruz. Since it was still early when I arrived, I was alone. I knelt in front of the altar and wept. I told the Lord all the sins I had committed, and then I asked Jesus Christ to come into my life. Dick, it was like a bolt of lightning hit me. I knew at once that I was free from evil spirits."

When I went for my next lesson, I brought Butch a modern English New Testament, and he read it through twice in as many weeks. He began telling his friends what had happened to him and warned them to stay away from Ouija boards. Evil spirits had entrapped him through playing with one. Butch joined a Campus Crusade group and began to grow spiritually and learned how to share his faith. The last time I saw Butch, he had led seven street kids to faith in Jesus.

When summer vacation came, we left Manila and returned to our regional translation center at Nasuli. By this time, I realized I would never be a guitarist. I had little talent for the instrument and was no longer interested in learning to play. But it didn't matter. God's sovereign purpose in my guitar lessons had come to eternal fruition. The guitar sitting in the corner was the instrument God used to bring Butch to faith in Jesus Christ.

# 21

# Mary Granaas

## 1978

In the late 1960s and through the 1970s, a middle-aged lady named Mary Granaas managed the Manila guesthouse for our organization. Because she cared for and prayed for all of us, she became our mentor.

Betty and I were there in the spring of 1978 with our co-translator, Rosito Lumansay. He was receiving radiation therapy at Philippine General Hospital for cancer of the larynx. Doctors told us that since Rosito's condition was terminal, radiation would give him only a few more months of quality life. Mary wonderfully cared for him and for us.

Some months later, I brought Rosito back for a checkup at the hospital, and an intern recommended chemotherapy. I felt uncomfortable about subjecting my dear brother in the Lord to the discomfort and malaise that chemotherapy would entail.

When Rosito and I arrived at the guesthouse, I asked Mary what she thought.

We sat down, and she prayed that God would give wisdom to the doctors and me about Rosito's treatment. She lifted her head and asked, "Why don't you call Dr. Roberta Romero?" Dr. Roberta was a Filipina physician and a gracious friend who had been instrumental in getting Rosito into the hospital as a charity patient.

When I called her, Dr. Roberta said, "The leading cancer surgeon in the country was my classmate in medical school. I'll ask him what he would suggest."

An hour or so later, she called and said, "Dick, I'm at the home of my physician friend, and, believe it or not, he knows all about Rosito." Some months before, all the cancer specialists in the country had held a special seminar to consider Rosito's case. They found it interesting because his type of cancer was rare among Filipinos.

"Dick, my surgeon friend says that if Rosito were his own father, he would not recommend chemotherapy," Dr. Roberta continued. "His recommendation in his own words was, 'Let the poor man go home and die in peace.'"

When I hung up the phone, I turned to Mary. "Thanks for praying. God has answered."

Rosito and I returned to our homes in the southern Philippines. He did die in peace but not before he held the first copy of the Manobo New Testament in his hands. Rosito, Betty, and I had worked together on that book for twenty years.

# 22

## The Last Pity Party

### 1978

In December 1978, Betty and I were in Pangi, our hilltop home among the Manobos. The New Testament translation had just been printed and would arrive in a week or so. It was cause for great joy, but we were concerned for our youngest son Dan. He was out of a job and was having a difficult time with life in the United States.

We should have rejoiced at the prospect of placing the Word of God in the hands of our Manobo friends, but on that particular morning, we had a pity party. The enemy whispered in our ears: *You've wasted your time and your lives. These people don't want this book you've produced. The Cebuano Scriptures are just fine for them, and that is really what they want. If you had stayed home in the United States and taken proper care of your son, you and he wouldn't be unhappy today.*

But God had not abandoned us. Later that morning, Mempiyanu, the lay pastor of the local Manobo church, and his wife, Iney Piyanu, arrived. These choice servants of God and dear friends came to pay a pastoral visit, and the Lord knew we needed it.

As we talked, I told them how we were feeling. "We're really discouraged, and the enemy is whispering in our ears," I said. "He is telling us to pack up and leave and never come back. We're not going to do that, but we need your prayers."

They were stunned. They assumed that because we were missionaries, we never became discouraged or tempted. (May the Lord forgive us for not being open enough for them to see us as we really were.) They didn't say much and soon left.

Iney Piyanu cried all the way home. "Old Deaf One," she said to her husband, "we should take care of this. Our brother and sister are hurting and need our prayers. Go tell our other brothers and sisters to come to our house so we can have a prayer meeting."

We don't know how many came or how long they prayed, but when we woke up the next morning, our hearts were again full of joy.

A few days later, we gathered in the little barrio chapel for the dedication service of the Manobo New Testament. Mempiyanu stood behind the stacks of beautiful new books and said to his people: "God has not called Father of Kathleen and Mother of Kathleen to evangelize the rest of our tribe. They have lived among us for many years and have given us this Book. We never dreamed we would have the Word of God in our language. It is like a shining star to us. Now it is time for them to move on and give some other people the Scriptures. God has not called them to stay and evangelize because, brothers and sisters, he has called us—you and me—to finish the task, and we are going to do it."

It was our turn to be stunned, but we were joyfully stunned. Mempiyanu's encouraging words were a total denial of what Satan had whispered in our ears.

We learned two important things from what he said. First, the little Manobo church members had matured, and they understood how to engage in spiritual warfare. Second, they now bid us good-bye with gratitude and true fellowship. It was time to go. These dear folks didn't need us any more, and others desperately needed our attention. God would lead us to the right people. We hiked back to Pangi that afternoon with joy and anticipation. Our pity party was over.

Mempiyanu's words to the church were prophetic. He eventually led a group of nine men who tramped the hills, selling the Scriptures and proclaiming the gospel in a hundred and twenty barrios and sitios.

Three years later, we began work among the Matigsalug, another Manobo group of Mindanao.

# 23

# A Day in the Lives of
# Two Bible Translators

## 1978

People often ask us, "What was it like when you were with the Manobo people? What occupied you on a typical day? What were your concerns, your burdens, your joys and pleasures?"

Come with me into the past, and walk through a typical day with the Elkins' family.

## Setting

We live in the heart of the island of Mindanao in the southern Philippines. Behind us is a nine-thousand-foot peak covered with rain forest, which the Manobos call the "Navel of the World." Since our house sits on a four-thousand-foot hill, we can gaze into four provinces on this island.

We are surrounded by farms and five or six houses belonging to our Manobo "brothers" and "sisters" and their families. They are all the children of Anggam Ramon, the highest chief of the tribe. He adopted us into his family in our early years here. Our house and airstrip are on his land.

Although we live in the tropics, the days are pleasantly warm with temperatures in the 80s, and the nights are chilly in the 60s. This is a little bit of paradise.

Our house, while ramshackle by Western standards, is comfortable. It has a galvanized iron roof and is built of lumber, hand cut in the nearby rain forest. Four fifty-gallon drums on a scaffold under the eaves collect rainwater, and piping brings it into a faucet over a metal kitchen sink. Since the rainy season lasts for seven to nine months, we usually collect enough water for our needs. An outhouse is connected to the house by a covered bridge.

## Schedule

A typical day goes something like this:

**5:15 a.m.** I get up and make a pot of locally grown coffee on our kerosene pressure stove. Then I take my Bible and steaming mug to the tiny front porch where I read and meditate while watching the sun rise through the mist over the mountains.

**5:45 a.m.** I turn on the shortwave radio to world news from Radio Australia. While Betty makes breakfast, I drape the mosquito net out of the way and make our bed.

**6:15 a.m. Breakfast.** Breakfast may be delayed, because as soon as we open the door, we may have company. Someone may need first aid, have a medical problem, or want to borrow a tool. Although we aren't medical professionals, we are equipped to deal with malaria, dysentery, pneumonia, intestinal worms, eye infections, cuts, and burns.

Our breakfast menu today consists of ripe papaya from one of our trees, fried eggs, recently harvested rice, and smoked pork. In the provincial capital market, we buy fresh pork, which we cure in salt brine and smoke. To prepare the meat, we boil out most of the salt then fry the pork. Delicious!

**6:30 a.m. Radio schedule.** This is a shortwave radio schedule with our translation center at Nasuli. The operator calls fifteen or more stations in alphabetical order. We are known by the call name "Pangi," the name of a fruit tree. Betty has a grocery list, so we check in and wait until more important message-traffic is cleared. Our director asks those of us in outlying areas to call in at least once a day as a precautionary measure. If we do not call in for three days, our director will send a JAARS plane to check on us. If we have unwanted armed visitors at an off-schedule hour day or night, we can activate a gadget on our radio that will turn on a radio at the center and transmit a call for help.

Having radio and air service is wonderful. During our first term, I spent almost a year—one week out of every month—in accumulated time just going out for mail and supplies. I often hiked the twenty-three miles between our village and the nearest public transportation. After Jungle Aviation and Radio Service (JAARS), an arm of our organization, began serving us, that week was shortened to about an hour and a half, then later to about twenty minutes. Can you imagine what the extra time means to a Bible translator?

This morning Betty calls in our grocery list. Then our colleagues, George and Valerie Hires in the nearby village of Mabuhay, ask to talk to us. They are the literacy team assigned to work with us here in Manobo country and are just learning the language. George wants me to come over and find out why the men won't let him work in the fields with them.

**7:00 a.m.** By now Betty has bread dough rising. Adriana, our "sister," comes to collect the laundry. She will wash it on the rocks at a nearby spring, then bring it home and hang it up. I spend a few minutes working in our garden and pick a few ripe papayas. Fruit trees are common property, but we insist that people pick only ripe fruit. Sharing is a social imperative here.

I settle down at my desk in my study (a small building in the backyard) for the day's work. I spend the first hour reading Manobo Scripture into my tape recorder. Iney Piyanu ("Mother of Piyanu") may come later to sing about her faith, so I can also record that for others to listen to on a cassette tape. She will sing a Manobo song in a special traditional way. Manobos have song forms for every situation, and the people always will listen to songs. We found that out when Siblian sang the Scriptures, using an epic song style. He eventually recorded about eight hours of the Scriptures sung in poetic form, which people all over the area listened to with intense interest.

**9:00 a.m. Translation begins.** My translation assistant is busy today with his corn harvest, so I push ahead by myself on a rough draft of the Gospel of Matthew. I just get started when Betty calls, "Dick, come in, please!" Betty never calls unless she needs help with visitors or a snake has slithered into our house, but I always find it frustrating to have my work interrupted. The Lord often has to remind me that the feeding of the five thousand was the result of a large crowd of needy people who upset the plans of Jesus and his disciples to rest for a while. A missionary's life must always be a balance of grace and truth.

I walk in to a full house, for we seldom get just one visitor. In Manoboland, people don't go anywhere by themselves. Iney Mayin has a toothache. I get out my simple dental tools and look in her mouth. No wonder she has a toothache! She has yawning holes in two molars. I clean them out, feeling like an amateur archaeologist. I can tell what she has been eating by digging through the layers in the holes. I find guava seeds and pieces of ground corn. I sterilize the holes with peroxide and Merthiolate and mix up zinc oxide powder with a clove-scented binder for a filling. She really needs a dentist, but that is out of the question. We find that these temporary fillings often last for months, even years.

**10:00 a.m.** The visitors leave, taking with them a few large papayas off our trees. When I planted the seedlings years ago, someone asked, "What are you going to do with all those trees? Only children and pregnant women eat ripe papaya!" I chuckle to myself when I see that same man taking his share. We never have any lack of people to eat our ripe papayas, and few of them are pregnant women or kids. I planted forty trees, so we'll have enough fruit, also.

I pour myself another cup of coffee and return to the study.

Betty goes back to her manual typewriter. In those days before computers, translation work required the repeated typing and proofreading of manuscripts. Betty uses her knowledge of New Testament Greek to help me prepare for translation sessions. But now she too is interrupted. Her bread dough, which has risen twice, is ready to bake.

I collect my thoughts and return to the Gospel of Matthew. I begin translating the Beatitudes in chapter 5: "Blessed are the poor in spirit" (v. 3). I realize right away that I can't render that literally. It would come out as, "Blessed are those who don't have much spirit power." In this culture, that would mean the power of an evil spirit.

While it is true in a sense that those who do not have demonic spirit power are blessed, that is not what Matthew meant when he wrote his Gospel. I read the commentaries and decide to try something that I hope means, "How blessed are those who know they are spiritually poor." When Saturnino, my translation assistant, is free to work, I will ask him what he thinks this means. We check by feedback. Translation has to be an accurate communication of the meaning of the original in the language of the people who will read it. Often we do not translate what it literally says but what it means. Otherwise, it may end up meaning something very different. I have no more interruptions before lunch. My goal for the day is twenty verses in rough draft.

**12:00 noon.** Betty calls me for lunch, which is rice, canned chopped beef, and *paku,* the tips of a wild fern that grows in damp places. Anggam Ramon brought it yesterday. We also have corn on the cob that his daughter gave us this morning when she brought back the laundry. We wash the dishes, shut the front door, and lie down for a short siesta. A few minutes of sleep add a couple of efficient hours to the end of my day.

**1:30 p.m.** I return to the study while Betty works ahead on the Book of Matthew, making notes for me to help speed up translation.

As soon as I sit down, I hear Andi and Tatu', the three- and four-year-old neighbor children, outside the study. They pause for a moment, talking quietly, then climb the ladder and push the door open with a bang. They walk in and stand in front of my desk.

I greet them in Manobo fashion. "So you have arrived, have you?"

"Yes, Uncle, we have arrived."

"Perhaps you have a purpose?"

Even at their early ages, they know it is not polite to blurt out what they want until a proper interval has passed. I ignore them for a while and return to work.

Before long, one of them speaks. "Uncle, make us airplanes." This is a common request.

I take pieces of scrap paper and make two paper airplanes.

Their mission accomplished, they hurry down the ladder and noisily fly their planes just outside. I know they will come back, teasing me repeatedly with additional requests until I say, "Enough! Go play somewhere far away!" And they will run away, giggling. We love these kids, and they are a comfort when our own children are away at school.

**2:30 p.m.** Bayi and Jesus, the parents of Andi and Tatu', come with a dilemma. Bayi's brother, Rosito, is terminally ill, with only a short time to live. Rosito is a devout believer, but his father, a powerful leader, is still an animist and follows the dictates of local spirits.

Recently, a local shaman consulted his spirits and reported that this illness is because Rosito did not consult the spirits of a nearby lake when he became a Christian. So they are punishing him with this illness. He will get well if a large pig is sacrificed to them.

Bayi and Jesus are believers and have a large pig. Rosito's father has asked them to give him the pig for the sacrifice. They are reluctant to give the pig for this purpose, but they are also reluctant to refuse to do so. Relatives have accused them of becoming Christians so they have an excuse for not helping in family affairs. They want to please God, but they also want to be seen as caring members of the family. This is important because these people are much more family-oriented than we are in the West.

So they come to us for advice. "What shall we do?" they ask.

What should we tell them? What is right in this situation? My American culture combined with my Christian background prompt me to tell them not to give the pig. But my acquired Manobo culture urges me to wait and think about it for a while. In this culture, a father has the right to take a pig from any of his children, especially from a son-in-law whose bride-wealth debt for a wife will never be fully paid. It is socially imperative for a son-in-law to help his father-in-law with whatever means he has at all times. This never varies.

"If the circumstances were different," I ask, "would you give the pig?"

"Of course. We could *never* refuse to help. It would be a terrible thing if we did."

After pondering a while, I say, "I think you should give your father the pig. He has a right to the pig, but what he does with it will be his own responsibility before God." We found out later that the other Manobo Christians agreed, but it helped Jesus and Bayi to hear it from me.

So Jesus and Bayi told her father he could have the pig. The church members prayed that God would either heal Rosito or take him to heaven before the pig could be sacrificed.

Two nights later, a few hours before the sacrifice was to take place, Rosito died and went into the presence of the Lord, and that ended the matter. The result, we all believed, was a much better statement to the father and other non-Christians than if they had refused him his rights for the pig. Later, Bayi's father came to Jesus before he died.

**3:30 p.m.** Meneminto and lay pastor Mempiyanu come to talk about a church problem. A believer has not been attending the services. What should they do about it?

Again, we have to be careful. Church discipline must be carried out in line with cultural patterns, but the first question should always be, What does Scripture say? We talk about it a while, referring to Galatians 6:1–2: "Brothers, if someone is caught in a sin, you who are spiritual should restore him gently. But watch yourself, or you also may be tempted. Carry each other's burdens, and in this way you will fulfill the law of Christ" (NIV).

Then Mempiyanu says, "Our tape player doesn't play anymore."

"Did you look inside?" I ask.

"Well, only a little peek."

I remove the cover and discover some thirty small cockroaches inside. I take it outside and blow them out. The wires to the battery box are broken, so I heat up my soldering iron on the kitchen stove and solder them. I replace the cover and give it back to them.

They also have a flashlight to be repaired, and I take care of that and mend a trade-language version of the New Testament. As I work on it, I pray that God will speed the day when they will have their own Manobo New Testament, one that they can clearly understand. They leave, taking along aspirin and worm medicine for their sick children.

**4:45 p.m. Afternoon radio schedule.** The pilot tells us he is making a flight tomorrow to bring our groceries and mail. Also, he will fly me over to Mabuhay, five minutes away, to see if I can find out why the men of that village will not let George Hires work in the fields with them. Several days ago, George had asked me to come. It is important for him to be with other men in order to learn Manobo. The pilot will also bring the pipe I ordered, all cut and threaded, from the shop at our center. I never do get back to translation today.

**5:15 p.m.** It is now near sundown. Anggam Ramon and his wife come over, and we sit on the front porch and talk until it is quite dark. Anggam has been a father to us all the years we have lived here. He and his wife are not yet believers, but they are wonderful people and have listened carefully to our explanation of the gospel. I firmly believe that when conversion takes place in any culture, it always involves a worldview change. These people have a lot farther to go than I did when I believed in Jesus. They borrow kerosene for their lamp and leave. I light our pressure lamp, and Betty gets supper.

As we finish eating, the only sounds we hear are a dog barking in the distance, the crickets chirping, an owl hooting in a nearby *baliti* tree, and the hissing of our pressure lamp. We read the Scriptures and pray together for each person who came to our door today, for our children away at school, for our colleagues who lovingly care for them at the center, and for folks back home who support us and pray for us.

Since these last hours of the day are without interruption, we work a while longer, reading the galley proofs of the Book of Acts. We read other books until we are too sleepy to hold them.

I turn off the hissing lamp. We crawl into bed and tuck the mosquito net around the mattress. The night sounds close in on us, and the day is over.

# 24

# A Promise Kept

## 1982

In April 1982, after almost thirty years in the Philippines, I was enjoying my first real office job as I served in administration at our field headquarters. We had translated the Manobo New Testament, and a team from the Translators Association of the Philippines was in Manobo country developing literacy programs and supervising the distribution of the New Testament.

By then, we lived in Manila, and my assignment provided academic liaison with scholarly and government institutions. I helped scholars at the Institute for Philippine Languages edit a new Filipino-English dictionary. Betty worked as secretary for the associate director for academic affairs and assisted the guesthouse manager. We enjoyed the fellowship of our colleagues and found life in a large Asian city interesting and exciting.

In the midst of our busyness, I almost forgot the promise I had made to Matigsalug Datu Mampangendey twenty-five years earlier. When I had first visited Matigsalug country, I said to him, "Uncle, we cannot come now, but I promise you that someday, if God makes it possible, we will move here and translate God's Word for your people."

Eventually, Betty and I dismissed the possibility of living among the Matigsalug because a translation team began working on the closely related Tigwa Manobo language. Survey results showed that these two speech varieties were mutually understandable, so we assumed the Tigwa Scriptures would be adequate for the Matigsalug people also.

However, one morning Betty and I received a letter from our director, Hart Wiens, asking if we would be interested in beginning a translation program for the Matigsalug. Two different mission organizations had asked him for a translation team for the Matigsalug area. Apparently, both missions found that various sociolinguistic issues caused the Matigsalug people to respond negatively to Scripture portions in the Tigwa Manobo dialect. Hart shared the letters with program specialist Kathy Bosscher, and they agreed that he should ask Betty and me to consider this assignment.

We were definitely interested. It seemed the world had turned right-side up again. Life in the city was good, but my heart was still in the mountains and valleys of Mindanao. It seemed to us the whole idea had the marks of sovereign Providence. Neither Hart nor Kathy knew anything about our past experience with the Matigsalug people nor the promise I had made so many years before.

In a few days, we answered Hart's letter, saying we would be happy to begin a translation project among the Matigsalug. We knew I would need to hike into Panganan, the village of Datu Mampangendey. The datu was no longer living, but I thought perhaps people there would remember me. We would need to renew friendships, ask for permission to live there, and, if possible, reopen the airstrip we had built in the early sixties.

A few months later, director Hart Wiens, pilot Dave King, Nasuli center administrator Pat Cochran, and I made the trip to Panganan. It was no longer a six-day hike to reach the village. Logging roads now penetrated the area, so we could travel in a four-wheel-drive vehicle to within a half-day's walk. We drove east to the Tigwa Manobo area and stopped in a village on the headwaters of the Salug River. We left our vehicle in the care of a local datu and set out on foot, following the river downstream. Overseas Missionary Fellowship (OMF) missionaries who worked in the area, Linda Hinchliffe and her friend, joined us for the hike.

Shortly before dark, we approached the crest of the hill overlooking the village. I stopped my companions and said, "What we find in the next few minutes is crucial. If the airstrip has been planted to corn, we may not be able to work here. But I really want to, because this is Datu Mampangendey's village, and I promised him I would return someday."

When we reached the top of the hill, we looked down at the village spread before us on the other side of the river. The airstrip was there—a well-defined, long patch of land running north and south through the middle of the village. We made our way down and crossed the river. People immediately recognized me. Someone shouted, *"Elukuy ni*

*Masulug!* The friend of *Masulug!*" (The word, meaning "plenty," was Datu Mampangendey's nickname because he had six wives.) I recognized three of the leading men as the teenage boys who had guided our rafts down the river twenty-five years before. They welcomed us warmly.

The people led us to an open thatched structure called the *sosiyal hol* (social hall) where we sat down. After a polite interval, Datu Umising, the leading man in the village, asked me, "Brother, why have you come?"

"Because of my promise to Uncle Mampangendey. When I came here many years ago, I promised him that some day my wife and I would live here and translate the Word of Manama [God] for the Matigsalug people. The time has come for me to keep that promise. I now ask your permission for my wife and me to come."

Datu Umising and the other men talked among themselves for a moment or two, then he said, "You are our brother, and we would gladly welcome you here, but we cannot give you permission. That can only come from Datu Gawilan, our supreme tribal chieftain who now lives in Sinuda. You will have to go there to see him. If he grants your request, you may come. If he refuses, we are sorry, but you may not come. If we can choose a day to meet in Sinuda, I can go with you to see him."

We agreed to meet the following Monday. The town of Sinuda was on the highway from Bukidnon to Davao City and could easily be reached by bus or jeepney.

Before we left, I asked Umising why they had not planted corn on the airstrip.

He said Mampangendey had given strict orders: "Some day my American son will return here to live. When he comes, he will need this airstrip, so you must never plant anything on it." He had also set aside an area for us to build a house.

After spending the night in Panganan, we hiked back to our vehicle and drove home.

The following Monday, Hart Wiens and Dr. Steve Lynip drove their motorcycles to Sinuda with me as a passenger. Umising was waiting for us. We all went together to the office of Datu Gawilan.

I reminded Datu Gawilan that he had visited us once during our first year in the Philippines. Now I introduced myself as Dr. Richard Elkins of the Summer Institute of Linguistics, but the Manobo people called me *Mangkaklin,* "Father of Kathleen." I also told him that his younger brother, Datu Ugtad Gawilan, had accompanied me to Salug country twenty-five years before.

I gave the datu copies of literacy materials we had prepared in Western Bukidnon Manobo—a short dictionary, a book of local folk tales, a world atlas, a health book, a primer, and a Manobo New Testament.

He picked up the New Testament, thumbed through it, and handed it back to me. "Read something," he said.

I chose the Christmas story in chapter 2 of Luke's Gospel and read it aloud.

Datu Gawilan turned to another datu who was his secretary and a Christian. "Is that how it should be?"

"Yes," the other man replied, "that is how it should be."

Datu Gawilan told his secretary, "Prepare a letter for Dr. Elkins, stating that he has full permission to live in Panganan to pursue his linguistic and philanthropic work among the Matigsalug people."

The secretary typed the letter with a number of copies and handed the original to Datu Gawilan to sign. He did so, put it in an envelope, and handed it to me.

With this important document in hand, I expressed our thanks to him and to the other officials and left. We said good-bye to Umising, who left on his two-day trek to Panganan. We rode back to Nasuli in a furious rainstorm, which was normal for mid-September.

At home that evening, I read the letter. It was short, to the point, and what I expected, except for one feature. The letter read, "This is to certify that Dr. Richard Elkins, alias *Datu Mangkaklin*, has full permission to live and work in Barrio Panganan to pursue his linguistic and philanthropic work among the Matigsalug people. [Signed] Datu Lorenzo Gawilan, Supreme Tribal Chieftain of the Matigsalug people."

The surprising feature was that the letter referred to me as *Datu Mangkaklin*. This was a new wrinkle. No one had ever called me a datu before. In Western Bukidnon, people address every parent by a teknonym, that is, a name beginning with "father of" or "mother of." Evidently among the Matigsalug, people address only datus by teknonyms. When I mentioned my teknonym, Datu Gawilan assumed I had achieved the status of datu among the Manobo people and had included this information in the letter. With tongue-in-cheek, I said to Betty, "I am now a datu and have a letter from the Matigsalug supreme tribal chieftain to prove it."

The letter itself was far more important than my doubtful new status; it was visible evidence that God was working. He certainly had not forgotten my promise so many years before and had sovereignly enabled us to keep it.

A few weeks later, Pat Cochran drove Betty and me to the village where we had left the truck previously. OMF missionary Linda Hinchliffe had arranged for rafts to be made for us, and these were ready. We had our personal effects, enough food for two weeks, our bedding, and a battery-operated radio transmitter and receiver. Betty, Pat, and I boarded the rafts with our equipment around noon and leisurely floated downstream.

It was almost evening when we arrived at Panganan. An overwhelming joy flooded over me at this fruition of a long-ago dream. The entire village ran down to the riverbank to welcome us.

We slept that night in a large vacant house that needed repairs. In spite of a rain, we managed to keep dry. Pat spent the night with us then left in the morning for home.

At first, we felt lonely, but that feeling quickly faded as people visited and brought fragrant new rice. Because everyone remembered that Mampangendey had adopted me as his "son," we soon found we had "relatives" everywhere. All were friendly and attempted to make us feel at home.

The Matigsalug people understood our Manobo better than we understood their speech, so we were able to share the gospel with them from the beginning. Their curiosity about us provided openings. For instance, an elderly woman asked me, "Aren't you afraid to sleep in that house?"

I was puzzled. "Why should we be afraid?"

"Many people died in that house," she answered. "Many ghoul spirits are around there."

"I'm not afraid of ghoul spirits. As a matter of fact, the ghoul spirits are afraid of me!"

This was a surprising thought to her, and her response might best be rendered, "Give me a break! That cannot possibly be true."

"It is true," I said. "Jesus, the Son of Manama, is my friend. He stays close by me and protects me. We know from the Book of Manama that the ghoul spirits were afraid of him. Because he is always with me, the ghoul spirits do not come near me."

Our most pressing task at first was to restore the airstrip. During our visit several weeks before, pilot David King had walked with me over the strip and suggested changes before the first landing. We needed to remove rocks, fill holes, and level the strip. Then we had to compact the surface so it could bear the weight of an aircraft. On this trip, we brought a roller made from a steel drum that could be filled with water. We hoped that if this were hitched to a water buffalo and pulled over the strip, it would make the surface firm enough. Datu Umising agreed to use his buffalo for the task.

We also brought several shovels and picks. On the second morning after our arrival, I began work with a pick and shovel. I thought if I had to work alone, our food would be gone before I was halfway finished. I needn't have been concerned.

In a few minutes, the entire village joined me. With great enthusiasm and camaraderie, men, women, and children spread out over the strip. Some cut grass with their bolos, some threw rocks off to the side, and others leveled humps and filled in low spots with picks and shovels. We repeated this process every morning for an hour until we had done an adequate job.

Now one of the pilots would have to hike out and take a look at it. Then he would call the center by radio and have a plane make a test landing. The village was in a deep valley, and the approach to the strip on both ends was short because of hills. One pilot told me later that it was the tightest strip he had ever landed on. How thankful we were for the Heliocourier and well-trained pilots.

Our next concern was where to live until we could arrange to build a house of our own. Datu Umising offered his tiny thatched house for our temporary use. It was eight feet wide by twelve feet long with a shaded porch and was divided into two small rooms. The inner room became our bedroom, kitchen, and dining space. I built a sleeping bench on one side and a shelf for our kerosene pressure stove for our kitchen. The space under the bed was for storage. We fastened a large plastic sheet with thumbtacks under the roof to keep cockroach droppings from falling on us and into our food. The outer room became our workspace and reception area for visitors. Cabin fever was not a problem because most of our living took place outside or on our shaded porch. I made the doors and windows lockable so we could come and go without worrying about items "walking off."

Two weeks after we arrived, Pat Cochran and a pilot drove out to the end of the road and hiked in to inspect the airstrip. The pilot then radioed his partner at Nasuli to fly out and land. The flight took only twenty minutes. The pilots made several landings and takeoffs, after which they declared that the Panganan strip was in service.

Since our larder was exhausted, Betty and I joined the flight back to Nasuli. We also realized we needed a break. We were experiencing much more culture stress than we had expected. Although many similarities existed between the Manobo people we had lived among for twenty-five years and these people, we soon discovered great differences. Our new friends were far more demanding and less apt to avoid confrontation. In our first two weeks among them, we were much more involved in village life than we had ever been with the Manobos.

We went to our center at Nasuli for a week but were eager to return. We had accomplished our goals for our first two weeks. We had a house to come back to, an airstrip to land on, and a friendly welcome awaiting our return. The prospect of serving the Lord among these wonderful people gave us a sense of purpose and joy.

Most important of all, we had kept my promise, a promise that we trusted would bring the Word of God and with it, new hope and new life to the people of this valley.

# 25

## House "Off Limits"?

### 1983

In the spring of 1983, the construction of our house in the Matigsalug village of Panganan was almost finished. Every afternoon, just before the carpenters stopped for the day, I climbed into the main part of the structure to see what had been accomplished.

Several days later, a number of our local friends joined me. We talked as we stood on the loose floorboards not yet nailed down.

"When all this is finished," a man said, "you won't want us Matigsalug people to come up to this part of the house."

I was stunned. "Why in the world do you say that?"

He looked down at his bare toes. "Well, we don't wear shoes, and the ground is muddy. You won't want us walking on this nice wooden floor with our muddy feet. We'd get it dirty."

"We don't care about that."

"The lowlanders don't let us Matigsalug people go into their houses," he added.

"We're not lowlanders."

"But what about mud on the floor?"

"We'll wipe it up."

The man paused then spoke in a determined voice. "No, we'll just stay down below. You can come and talk to us, but we won't come up into your house."

All eyes turned on me.

"If that's the case," I said, "then we'll know you don't really consider us to be your Matigsalug brother and sister." I searched their faces to see if they understood. "Tell me, which is easier—to wipe away a little bit of mud on the floor or to wipe away a big pain in a brother's breath because we don't think he's good enough to come into our house?"

The men were silent.

A few weeks later, we moved into our new home.

We made everyone welcome, and we all enjoyed the house together.

# 26

# God Answers Prayer for Punsu

## 1986

In 1986, an SIL (Summer Institute of Linguistics) dictionary-making workshop was hosted at the center at Nasuli. Most people attending were Wycliffe translators, but we were delighted that several prominent Filipino linguists from the Institute for Filipino Languages were also with us. When linguistic and translation work first began in the Philippines, this organization offered us office space in Manila. Over the years, a number of their people had become our close friends.

During the workshop, I spoke to our director Hart Wiens, suggesting that it would be good if our friends could visit one of our projects as a public-relations gesture. I further suggested that the village of Panganan where Betty and I were working would be ideal for the visit. Since it was close by, our plane could reach the airstrip in about twenty minutes. I felt, however, that I should go out a day early to make sure that no insurgent group was operating in the area. It would not be wise if our friends, being important government officials, were exposed to this kind of risk.

Hart agreed with my suggestions, and we made plans for the flights out to Panganan.

On the day before the planned visit, the pilots flew me out ahead. Usually when we landed, our good friend, Datu Umising, came to meet the plane, but after we touched down this time, his older brother, Dikuy, greeted us.

"Where is Umising?" I asked.

"Big trouble! Punsu is dying. Please come and see him."

Punsu was Datu Umising's six-year-old son. He had been only two years old when we first came to live in Panganan, and we loved him like one of our own kids. He was a fun-loving, well-behaved child, friendly, and something of a clown. He had been sick with malaria a couple of weeks before, and we had treated him for it. Evidently, he had had another attack.

I handed my keys to the pilots and asked them to make themselves at home in our house. I needed to see if I could do anything for Punsu and his family.

Dikuy led me to his home, and we climbed up the notched-log ladder into the house. When I saw Punsu, I was deeply distressed. His father, Umising, was sitting on a sleeping bench holding him on his lap. The child seemed comatose. Although his eyes were open, he was unaware of anyone around him. My guess was that he was suffering from cerebral malaria. They told me that he had been this way for three days and had not eaten or drunk anything during that time. I decided I would send a note with the pilots to Dr. Steve Lynip, our physician at the center. He might have a suggestion and could send some medicine when the plane returned with the visitors the next day.

After I told Umising and his wife what I intended to do, I started to leave.

Umising shook his head. "No, brother, pray for him first!"

I knelt down, placed my hand on the child, and said to his parents, "I will have to speak in English. I am too upset to pray in Matigsalug." For about five minutes, I pleaded with the Lord, asking him in the strong name of Jesus to heal the child and restore him to full health to his parents and to all of us.

When I finished praying, I took my leave, climbed quietly down the ladder, and returned to the plane where the pilots were waiting to take off to return to Nasuli. Before they left, I handed them a note for Dr. Steve.

With an anxious heart, I went to our house. It was about noon, so I ate part of the lunch I had brought with me—cold rice and beans cooked with Vienna sausages. Then I felt I should go back to be with Umising and his wife and see if I could do something more.

As I ascended their ladder, I heard people inside talking excitedly. I had just reached the doorway when Umising greeted me with a joyful shout: "Brother! God has healed him!"

I looked over to the sleeping bench where Punsu had been lying. He was sitting up, wide-awake, and his mother was feeding him. He looked perfectly normal. I joined in the general rejoicing and praised God for hearing our prayers. God had indeed healed this much-loved child, and we were all ecstatic.

I looked at the meager meal he was having and quickly went home to get the remains of my lunch. The child needed something more sustaining than what he was eating. When I returned, our jubilee of thanksgiving continued as we watched Punsu gobble down what I had brought.

Later that afternoon, he played outside with the other children, and to all appearances he was completely normal. Actually, in the weeks that followed, he was more robust and healthy than he had been for a long time.

The visitors arrived the next day, and I spent a couple of hours showing them around the village. It was a good visit, and our Manila friends thoroughly enjoyed the welcome our Matigsalug friends gave them.

Later that evening back at Nasuli when I told Betty what had happened, we both agreed that God had a reason for the trip beyond our idea of public relations. His love and mercy for a six-year-old boy showed the Matigsalug people that he loved them and wanted them to be his own.

# 27

# Whose Tin Roof Was It, Anyway?

## 1986

The thatched roof of the social hall in Panganan, the Matigsalug village where we were doing Bible translation work, leaked badly. So when we replaced the galvanized-iron roofing sheets on our house at the translation center at Nasuli, we offered the old sheets to the village leaders. We had the sheets flown out and stacked in the social hall to wait for the people's workday.

A day or so later, I noticed that Dikuy, my "brother-in-law,"[17] was roofing his house with used galvanized sheets, and his house was next to the social hall. He was a strong-willed person with much clout in the area, so I suspected he was using the roofing we had brought to the village. He often referred to his relationship with me as a good reason why we should give in to his frequent requests that we share our "wealth" with him.[18]

Upset and perplexed, I wondered, *Could he possibly feel he has a right to some of the sheets? What should I do about this?* Because of my American propensity to "fix" things, I felt I should do something. *Most Matigsalug*

---

17   He was the son-in-law of Datu Mampangendey, who had adopted me as his "son" in 1957 during my first trip to Matigsalug country. This made me his "brother-in-law."

18   In Matigsalug country, interpersonal relationships brought many obligations we Westerners didn't understand. We had much to learn about finding our way through the maze of cultural complexities.

*people hate confrontation,* I thought. *Since the roofing came from us, everyone will expect me to deal with him.*

Reluctantly and with increasing resentment, I ambled over to where he was nailing the sheets on his roof. "Hey, Uyang,"[19] I called, "your new roof looks very nice."

He answered but could probably sense that I was upset about the roofing and had come to talk about it. He smiled rather smugly but didn't say anything more and went on with his work.

*What a rascal!* I thought. *He's going to try to brazen his way through this.*

But then I took a good look at the sheets he was using and realized they were not the ones we had brought. Evidently, he had gotten them elsewhere and had been saving them to roof his house after he had made repairs. But why did he decide to use them at this time? Was he just trying to "get my goat"? He had certainly done that.

I complimented his work again, and after a polite interval, I walked back to our house. I was still puzzled about it, but after thinking carefully through the whole incident, the truth dawned on me.

Matigsalug people have different but definite ideas about rights over personal property. Dikuy wisely had counted the sheets we had brought out and decided there were not enough to cover the social-hall roof. Unless his were nailed down on his own house, the village men would surely ask him to offer his for the project. Refusing would be virtually impossible because local constraints about sharing made it difficult to refuse anyone. Ideas about personal property in his society were much looser than in ours, and to be considered stingy was social suicide. However, once he had his sheets nailed down on his roof, the pressure on him would be negligible.

I realized that the real problem was with me. We Americans are obsessed with making things right. If I had rushed to fix a situation I didn't understand, I would have lost a valuable friend. That would have been a much greater loss than the roofing material that was no longer ours anyway.

Later, when I understood my neighbors better, I realized that my "brother-in-law" couldn't possibly have gotten away with taking roofing that now belonged to the village. His fellow villagers would have dealt with him without my help.

The lesson is this: Whenever you're in a cross-cultural situation, you must do everything possible to understand the patterns of behavior in

19   *Uyang* is the Manobo term for a man's brother-in-law.

that society. When you think you understand, think again before you act. Be content to listen, observe, and let the locals deal with their problems without your interference.

In the final analysis, this situation really wasn't my problem. Fortunately, it wasn't anyone's problem.

# 28

# An Interrupted Sunday-School Lesson

## 1987

One Sunday morning in Panganan, Betty and I joined a large group crowded into the little grass-roofed chapel.

I had learned to be somewhat prepared because often, without warning, the leader would ask me to teach the Sunday-school lesson. This was one of those times. I taught from a rough-hewn pulpit set upon a post embedded in the dirt floor.

Suddenly, a commotion outside caused all eyes to shift from me to a scene developing a few hundred feet away. Three men hurried toward the chapel, carrying a struggling and screaming teenage girl. A screaming older woman was running alongside.

People in the chapel dashed outside where they huddled together at a distance, watching through the open front door.

Betty and I remained alone in the chapel.

The men ran in through a doorway behind the podium and dropped the girl onto the platform behind me.

The woman, the girl's mother, rushed in also and pounded me on the shoulder. *"Ampuim pa! Ampuim pa!"* ("Pray for her! Pray for her!") she shouted.

I knelt down, placed my hand on the frenzied girl's shoulder, and called upon the Lord in Matigsalug. "Our Father," I prayed, "I don't know what the problem is with this dear girl, but you know everything.

You know our thoughts, our fears, and our anxieties. You know what is frightening these people.

"If there is something evil that has attacked her and her family," I prayed, "I ask you now in the strong name of Jesus, your Son, to drive it away. Place a wall of your power around her, and give her and these people your peace. Remove their fear, and restore this young woman, I pray. Thank you that we can trust in your help and defense. In Jesus' strong name, amen."

When I began praying, the girl was struggling violently, but as I continued, her agitation ebbed away, and she became completely calm.

The men released their grip on her arms and legs, and she sat quietly on the floor.

I looked at the girl's mother. "You can take her home now."

"Oh, no!" she said. "She wants to stay and hear the Word of God."

The people filed slowly back into the chapel, and I resumed teaching. The atmosphere in the building was as peaceful again as if the frantic agitation of a few moments before had never happened.

I was a bit distracted by the possibility that the young lady sitting behind me on the platform might become hysterical again, but she remained calm and attentive.

The next day, we learned the cause of her disquiet. She had a grandmother who doted on her. A few days before, the grandmother was harvesting rice in a village upstream when she became stricken with cholera and died.

The Manobo people of Mindanao believe that sometimes the spirits of deceased persons return to this world to cause illness and death to beloved children or grandchildren so those children may join them in the world of the dead. This belief had caused the girl's fear and hysteria. She likely was also under demonic attack. We know the enemy often works to keep people under bondage to his lies. But it was obvious that God in his love and mercy had intervened and rescued her.

The Lord Jesus came to destroy the works of the devil, who holds such sway over these beautiful people of the Salug River Valley. Someday this dark influence will be broken.

The writer of the Book of Hebrews said, "Since the children have flesh and blood, he too shared in their humanity so that by his death he might destroy him who holds the power of death—that is, the devil—and free those who all their lives were held in slavery by their fear of death" (Hebrews 2:14-15 NIV).

The incident troubled me, and shortly afterward, I wrote the following poem.

**Dark Valley**
By Richard E. Elkins

The valley now is silent,
The night is mild and warm,
The darkness swiftly settles,
The hills are without form.

The nearby river murmurs,
The night winds softly sigh,
And in the vaulted heaven,
The ageless stars drift by.

Now westward drops red Baga,[20]
Belatik[21] follows near.
Above the eastern hillside,
Bright Lepu`[22] rises clear.

This is a lovely valley
As fair by night as day
When dawn appears with brightness
And burns the mist away.

But here in this fair valley
Where every scene delights,
There dwells a deeper darkness
Than all earth's moonless nights.

That darkness holds no splendor.
Its rule is fear and dread.
Long ages valley people
Have walked as live, yet dead.

Each dawning brings no freedom.
No shaman's secret rite
Can drive away the darkness,
This all-pervading night.

---

20   The red star in Taurus
21   Orion's belt and sword
22   Probably Vega, a bright star in Lyra

They call upon Kallayag[23]
To watch each grain-blessed field.
But it is not Kallayag
Who gives the bounteous yield.

They listen for Limuken,[24]
The spirit-omen bird.
But it is not Limuken
Who speaks the truthful word.

Nor is it Meivulan,[25]
Their sovereign most severe.
False is his rule of darkness.
He binds them fast with fear.

Lord God of hidden rivers,
Through dusk and gloom you see,
Peer down into this valley
And bid this darkness flee.

So banish cruel Kallayag,
Limuken put to flight.
No longer let Meivulan
Lead people into night.

Let truth dispel the darkness,
This valley fill with light.
Make plain the pure Evangel.
Turn blindness to clear sight.

Let dawn rise up with sweetness,
And people then will see
What darkness long had hidden,
And then they will be free.

---

23  The rice god
24  The omen bird is a species of dove.
25  Chief of the demons

# 29

# God, Saturnino, and the Communists

## 1983

Although we had begun the Matigsalug project now, we still enjoyed frequent contact with our Manobo friends. One afternoon, Pastor Saturnino Linog, one of our co-translators, arrived at our translation-center home at Nasuli.

When he saw me, he wept as he climbed the stairs to our front porch. I could see that he was greatly disturbed.

"*Geli*, what in the world is the matter?" I asked.

He tried to control himself. "All my neighbors have joined the New People's Army. They say if I do not join them, they will kill me, my wife, and our two small boys!" The New People's Army was an arm of the Communist party in the Philippines. Through his tears, he continued. "The world is no longer a nice place to live, is it, *Geli*? Please tell me what to do."

Betty and I were stunned. What should we tell our beloved brother in the Lord? We had never had our lives threatened like he had. Was it right to utter a few spiritual-sounding banalities? We felt completely unqualified to advise and comfort him.

We told our prayer partners, Paul and Alice Meisner, who were teachers at the center's elementary school, what had happened. That evening they joined us for prayer. We asked the Lord to rescue and protect Saturnino and his family.

The next morning, Betty and I prepared a box for him to take home—canned goods, dress fabric for his wife, and candy and cookies for his boys.

We were on the front porch as Saturnino got ready to leave. I said, "*Geli,* if what I say now is not true, then nothing I have ever told you is true nor is the Bible true. I say to you as strongly as I know how that your life cannot end until God calls you home. Someday he will say, 'Saturnino, my son, the work I had for you to do on earth is finished, and now I want you to come home to me.' But until that day comes, neither the Communists nor anyone else can touch you. You must remember this: unless God allows it, they cannot harm you, your wife, or your two boys. You are in his hands, and he is your protector."

We watched Saturnino walk away to catch a bus and wondered what he would face when he got home.

We heard no more for several days. Then his nephew arrived at the center. When we asked about Saturnino, he said, "You will not believe Uncle Saturnino! He has become fearless. On Sunday he stood at the pulpit of the church armed with his bolo [a long machete used for chopping or combat]. He preached against the Communists and even went to the municipal center and consulted the officials."

Again we were stunned. We felt like the country preacher who, with his congregation, prayed for rain, and a day later, sitting on the roof of his house in pouring rain, floating down the river, he looked up and said, "Lord, we prayed for rain, but this is ridiculous!"

We heard the rest of Saturnino's story later. The Armed Forces of the Philippines moved a detachment of soldiers into the municipality where Saturnino lived. They brought a field-artillery piece, and as a show of force, fired randomly into unoccupied areas on the hillsides. In short order, all of Saturnino's neighbors left the New People's Army and became loyal citizens again of the Philippine government. As far as we know, no further confrontation with the New People's Army took place in that part of the province.

God's ultimate purposes can never be frustrated. Saturnino was and is part of his purpose for people in that area of the Philippines. He and his family are as safe as God's eternal purpose is sure. Obviously, Saturnino learned that better than we did.

Today Pastor Saturnino is part of the team working on the translation of the Western Bukidnon Manobo Old Testament.

# 30

# Good-bye

# 1992

A few days before we left Mindanao in May 1992 to return to the United States for health reasons, two dear Manobo friends came to our center at Nasuli to say good-bye. They were Mempiyanu and Iney Piyanu, husband and wife, who were two of the first in their village to believe in Jesus.

Mempiyanu had been an alcoholic, and he and his wife had been deeply ensnared by the old animistic religion under bondage to evil spirits. Christ had totally changed their lives. Mempiyanu later became the lay pastor and served his people for many years.

On this particular day, they rode a bus from their village to our center and came to our house. We invited them to sit down. After a polite interval, Mempiyanu turned to us with a piercing look and pointed to his eyes. "The reason we have come today is because these eyes had to see your faces, and these ears had to hear your voices once more. You brought us the good news about Jesus. And where would we be today if you had not come?"

I was so emotionally overwhelmed that I could hardly speak.

They said little more and did not stay long.

After they left, I reflected on what Mempiyanu had said. It is true that Betty and I were privileged to be the visible ones to bring the gospel to their corner of Manoboland. But we were not the only ones. A host of people at home supported us and prayed for us. Our colleagues in the Philippines stood behind and helped us—radio technicians, pilots, schoolteachers, children's home parents, secretaries, builders, administrators, fellow translators, literacy experts, and others. Our faithful colleagues labored with us for many years and also brought the gospel to the Manobo people. It took a large team to make bright inroads into the darkness in which our Manobo friends lived.

We later learned that both Mempiyanu and Iney Piyanu had gone to be in the presence of their Savior. Someday in the courts of eternity, they and many other Manobo friends will fix their eyes on the faces of all who had a part in their enlightenment. Their gaze will be with new, eternal eyes, and they will understand more fully what it took to bring the Light to them.

And we will all rejoice together.

# 31

# Return to Barandias

# 2000

In the fall of 2000, Betty and I returned to the Philippines to revise the Western Bukidnon Manobo New Testament with Pastor Saturnino Linog for a second printing.

On December 22, we drove to the village of Barandias, where we had spent twenty-five years with the Manobo people. Our companions were Dr. Steve and Karen Lynip, longtime friends of ours and of these people. Steve had ministered medically to our former co-translator, Rosito, when he was dying of cancer in 1978.

The hour-and-a-half drive on paved roads contrasted sharply with the three-to-four-hour trips on dirt roads of twenty years earlier. We covered the last thirty-three kilometers on this day in about forty minutes. The scenery seemed more beautiful than I remembered.

When we first saw Barandias years ago, it was a small village of about twelve grass-roofed houses. It lay in the foothills of the nine-thousand-foot peak called Kalatungan. The village was the social center for about fifty Manobo families who practiced shifting cultivation in the rain-forested areas nearby.

Today the Manobo people are in the minority. People whose parents came from all over the Philippine Islands now occupy the village and the surrounding land. The rain forest is gone, replaced by sugar cane and cornfields. The Manobo people earn scant wages by weeding sugar-cane fields.

When we arrived this time, we found a new church building. I thought back to the first little grass-roofed church that was twelve-feet wide and fifteen-feet long. The new cement-block structure was much larger. A galvanized-iron roof covered the walls, giving it adequate protection from rain and the sun. Because we arrived in December, the church was decorated with tissue-paper stars hanging in the windows and a sign in English reading, "Merry Christmas."

The church was packed with bright eager faces. As we looked over the congregation, we realized that many people of our acquaintance had died. The youngsters we knew years ago were now old.

But we did recognize features of people now gone in the faces of the youths. One young woman joined three others in singing a Manobo hymn. Her lovely face reflected the beauty of her godly grandmother, who had prayed for us and lifted our spirits with her encouragement.

The young pastor gave a welcoming speech, and the congregation sang two songs led by another young man, who, we learned, was the son of Marcos, our younger "brother." Rosito, our co-translator, had translated those hymns several years before he died. I had a difficult time keeping back the tears as we sang. Then two visiting Manobo pastors told how they came to Christ years ago.

Following another musical number, the pastor asked me to speak. I struggled at first, as I had not spoken to a Manobo crowd for twenty years. Thankfully, I soon warmed to my task and read the familiar Manobo Scriptures as I preached.

After the service, we adjourned to a nearby house where women served us a meal of rice, noodles, and chicken adobo. We enjoyed sipping fresh coconut juice on straws through tiny holes cut in green coconuts.

Two smiling young ladies served our food, and one said, "You don't recognize us, do you?"

We shook our heads. "No, I don't," I said, and Betty agreed. We were amazed to learn that they were our "nieces" who grew up near us years ago and were often in our home.

It is hard to describe our feelings as we laughed and talked with these beautiful people, young and old. The gospel had lifted them from their former misery and given them hope.

After the meal, I talked with several men and the visiting pastors. One asked me to go and pray with Minggen, our younger "brother" who suffered from a long-time disorder. Before leaving, I gathered with our closest "relations" for prayer. They urged me to pray that the church would grow and that many who had heard the gospel would believe in Jesus.

In the old days after a service, Betty and I climbed to our hilltop home in Pangi on the land of our adopted father, Datu Lumansay, along with other members of his family. On this day, I wanted to climb that hill again and "go home" as we used to do, but we could no longer do that. After all, none of the family lived there any longer. Where our house once stood was now a sugar-cane field.

As we drove away, I said, "I wish we could do more to help these dear people."

Dr. Steve replied, "You and Betty did help them. You gave them the best gift of all—the Word of God."

# 32

# Escorts to Heaven

## 2000

One day during our stay in the Philippines in 2000, our Manobo friend Dionisia came to our home. When Betty and I invited her to sit down with a cup of tea, she asked, "Father of Kathleen, Mother of Kathleen, if a person accepts Jesus just before he dies, will he go to heaven?"

"Yes," I said. "Remember the criminal crucified next to Jesus? He expressed his faith as he was dying, and Jesus promised that he would be in heaven that very day."

"Oh, yes, that's right!" Dionisia said. "I had forgotten."

"Why do you ask?"

Then she told us about her nephew, a young man who was not a believer. He was walking by her house one day when another young man leaped out from some bushes, stabbed him with a knife, and fled.

Dionisia ran out and cradled her stricken nephew in her arms. "Trust Jesus!" she pleaded. "Ask him to save you, and you will go immediately to live with him in heaven."

"Yes, Auntie, I will trust him," whispered the young man. With a last feeble breath, he was gone.

Dionisia leaned forward. "That night," she said, "I dreamed my nephew came to me and took me by the hand. 'Auntie,' he said, 'you are going to escort me to heaven.'

"We began walking slowly upward. We soon came to a place with beautiful trees, flowers, and a stream. Everything was more wonderful than anything I had ever seen before.

"My nephew turned to me and said, 'Thank you, Auntie. You brought me to heaven.'

"The dream ended, and I woke up," she said. "Was God trying to tell me something true?"

I nodded my head. "Yes, it was something true."

After Dionisia left, we talked about her story. We agreed that when we lead persons to faith in the Lord Jesus, we surely are escorting them toward heaven.

# 33

# How Skillful God Is!
## 2001

Dionisia was our daughter Kathleen's playmate when they were children. Later, she became the wife of a young man who often helped us. She had the gift of evangelism, for in her sweet quiet way, she had led many to faith in Christ. One day in January 2001, just before we returned to the States, Dionisia came to the center at Nasuli to say good-bye.

After the Manobo New Testament had been published, Dionisia helped distribute it. Finally, all the copies were sold, but people kept asking for more. So she prayed that Betty and I would come back to the Philippines to prepare a new edition. When we returned in 2000, she knew that her prayers had been answered. In fact, she understood the power of prayer in all aspects of her life.

When we visited with her, I asked, "How is your brother Urbano?"

She seemed surprised. "Didn't you know that he died?"

"No. How did that happen?"

"He became ill several years ago," she said. "He went to a hospital in Cagayan, but he got worse. He died there alone, and his body was taken to the city morgue."

Then she explained that when she, her sisters, and her mother were notified, they traveled from their village some distance away and went to the morgue.

The morgue manager seemed gruff. "Where is your coffin and truck?" he asked.

"We have no truck," Dionisia said. "We have no coffin, and we have no money."

"You can't just leave the body here!" the manager retorted. "If you don't take it away by 3:00 o'clock tomorrow afternoon, you will all go to jail!"

"God will provide for us," Dionisia replied.

These women were destitute. Since they had no money and no food, they spent the night sitting outside the morgue, crying and pleading with the Lord to help them.

The next morning when Dionisia and her relatives still didn't have the means to take the body away, the manager became abusive.

The women told him again that the Lord would come to their rescue, but the hours passed slowly.

Other people joined the manager with their abuse.

Just before three o'clock, a little Catholic nun drove up in a truck. She climbed out and asked the women, "Are you in trouble?"

Dionisia replied, "Yes, we are." Then she told about their praying and trusting God to help them with this big problem.

"Last night I couldn't sleep," the sister said. "Suddenly, an angel appeared to me and said, 'Get a truck and a coffin and go to the morgue.' So now I'm here to help."

The nun and the women placed Urbano's body in the coffin and slid it into the back of the truck.

Before they left the morgue, the astonished manager asked the women's forgiveness. "I'm sorry," he said. "Indeed, God has come to your rescue."

The women drove the body to the cemetery where they held a short burial service.

Afterwards, the nun gave the women food and money and sent them home.

As Dionisia finished her story, Betty and I were speechless.

She looked at us and smiled. "How skillful God is!" she said.

Time and again, God showed his skillfulness in ordering the steps of two Bible translators and the people with whom they served.

# Epilogue

Betty Thumlert Elkins

Betty was born on Orcas Island, Washington, on March 13, 1927, and grew up on Seattle's Capitol Hill. We were married at Tabernacle Baptist Church in Seattle on August 19, 1949. After a brave battle with cancer, she went to be with the Lord on August 9, 2008, at our home in Albuquerque, New Mexico.

Betty shared a heavy load in our linguistic and translation work. While we translated the Manobo New Testament, she typed dozens of manuscripts on a manual typewriter and made hundreds of decisions about how a previously unwritten language should be spelled and punctuated.

She also brought to the translation desk her knowledge of New Testament Greek. To facilitate my labors, she worked ahead of me on the biblical text, looking up and typing the meanings of difficult Greek expressions and pertinent parts of commentaries.

A skilled typist, she prepared an error-free, photo-ready copy of our *Manobo-English Dictionary* for publication at the University of Hawaii Press (1968). As a proofreader, she had an uncanny eye for detail.

Betty also taught preliterate Manobo women to read fluently, using a primer we wrote. This sparked a desire among the men to learn to read too, which they did.

Her organizational, financial, and clerical skills were not only valuable for our project but also for our organization in general. She served several times as guesthouse hostess and as secretary to the director of the Philippine branch of our organization. For a number of years, she was the executive secretary for our teaching staff, which trained Asian Bible translators in the Philippines, India, and at the Asia Summer Institute of Linguistics in Singapore.

Betty was a competitive tennis and ping-pong player and a good cook. She was also a devoted mother to our three children—Kathleen, Tom, and Dan. Her weekly letters to them were often their only lifelines to us in an age before e-mails or cell phones.

Then too she was a woman of prayer. The children knew we prayed for them daily. When she was gone, their sense of loss for a prayer warrior was deep. She collected e-mails and prayer letters from friends and family and integrated all the requests. Every day we prayed for different ones.

For the fifty-nine years of our marriage, Betty was my best friend and loving wife.

A gifted speaker and writer, she left behind a treasure of information and wisdom not only in print but also in the hearts and lives of those she touched around the world.

In her own words, here are some of Betty's stories:

## Little Did I Know

From ages six to fourteen, I remember walking to Tabernacle Baptist Church in Seattle, Washington, five blocks away from our home—rain or shine. Little did I know then that hiking would be a big part of my life in the Philippines—rain or shine.

My mom never missed attending church if she could help it. Her example instilled in me the importance of group worship. I couldn't have guessed that someday I would set an example to people who worshipped their spirit gods only when they wanted a good rice harvest or were sick.

When I was young, I often played hymns as piano solos at church. I didn't know then that I would often accompany group singing at our translation center on Mindanao in the Philippines.

I sat next to a close friend at church the night we both gave our hearts to Christ. We were baptized at the same time and sang duets together. Ours was one of the lifetime friendships and partnerships made in the church that would support our future Bible translation work.

When I was old enough, I sang in the church choir. On the basis of that experience, I was accepted into the choir when I attended Westmont College in Santa Barbara, California. The choir tours became spiritual highlights during my college years.

Pastor Forrest Johnson and his wife were dignified, stalwart, loving messengers of the truth. They laid down solid scriptural principles that I drew on over and over again.

Near the end of my high-school years, our pastor brought a message of commitment not only to Christ but also to taking the gospel message to the world. Again and again, I was led to reconsider my priorities. I had only a dim realization that I was being prepared for future ministry.

A couple in our church had attended Westmont College, and when I was in high school, they showed me their yearbook. Almost immediately, I knew that was where I was to study. Little did I know then that the course of my life would be determined by decisions I made at Westmont.

Some leaders of the Navigators and Young Life organizations were members of our church too. The summer before I left for college, I worked for Lorne Sanny, who later became general director of the Navigators. The lessons of faith in God's provision that I saw there would serve me the rest of my life.

Dick and I were married at Tabernacle Baptist in 1949. The church sent us to the Philippines in 1953, and Pastor Johnson later baptized two of our children. The church was a faithful part of our financial and prayer support for forty-two years.

Little did I know as a six-year-old that this church and its people would be part of me forever—in this life and the next.

## Just a Little Can of Ham

I'll be honest. I was hoarding a two-pound can of ham under our bed. You see, generosity does not come naturally to me. I was young, our southern center in the Philippines was only a year or two old, and our family was there for a short period before returning to the village. I hid the treasure away in our little two-room bamboo cottage for a future family celebration.

Other Wycliffe members were at the center too. Since Thanksgiving was approaching, we women met to decide what to bring for our group meal. We had plenty of local items—chicken, potatoes, squash for pies, vegetables, and salad makings. But what would make the dinner "special" for Thanksgiving? Someone offered olives; another offered a can of cranberry sauce; and still another offered a package of dried mincemeat.

While this was going on, I was quiet, but I was saying to myself and reasoning with God, *I intended that we would use our little ham in*

*Barandias just for the four of us, not a big group of fifteen or twenty people. We'd hardly get a taste of it if I offered it for Thanksgiving.* Everyone else had offered something. I was the last to speak. Finally, very grudgingly, I said, "We'll bring a small ham for dinner."

Thanksgiving Day came. Since the ham was cold, I was able to cut it in thin slices that served everyone. We all enjoyed a delicious meal.

In January, we received a large package from the States that had been mailed two months before Thanksgiving. The senders were supporters, but they had never sent us a package before nor had even written. To our amazement, inside were six cans of ham weighing five pounds each!

From then on, whenever anyone talked about selfishness or generosity, I pictured a little can of ham hidden under our bed. When I offered it to others, even grudgingly, God exchanged it for a gift fifteen times larger. He gave me a lesson in eternal values that I will never forget.

## The Mountain of Mud

In 1965, I started testing our primer to see if I could use it to teach Manobo people how to read. I conducted a women's class of beginners five days a week for three months. Then for another three months, I had them read for practice to cement what they had learned.

My only problem—the class was an hour away from our home in Barandias. That meant six months of daily hiking with seventeen ups and downs over muddy trails. Dick later figured that I had hiked the equivalent of a climb from sea level to the top of Mt. Everest and back down by the time the six months was over. I often wondered if it was worth it all.

The Manobo women had been thrust into the midst of the majority Filipino culture that infiltrated the area. They often felt insecure and inferior to sophisticated women with their finer dresses and modern hairstyles.

During one class, the women read aloud one by one, "Be beautiful inside, in your hearts, with the lasting charm of a gentle and quiet spirit, which is so precious to God" (1 Peter 3:4). They stopped reading and exclaimed in affirmation by making clicking sounds at the back of their tongues. Some women even had tears in their eyes.

They had given me bananas, sweet-potato tops, corn, and new rice as tokens of appreciation—the best in material goods they had to offer. But those gifts were nothing compared to the beautiful sounds of affirmation of the truth they'd read for themselves. The Scripture hit home. For the first time, they realized that inner beauty is precious in God's sight.

And for me? The mountain of mud was suddenly just a little puddle.

# Afterword

Agnes Lawless Elkins
A final word from Dick Elkins

In 1957, John and Agnes Lawless came to the Philippines to join the work Wycliffe Bible Translators had recently begun there. Agnes ("Atchie") began a little school and taught our children, and John was our first radio technician. They not only were our neighbors at the center on Mindanao, but they also became our close friends. After a number of years of fruitful ministry, they returned to the United States due to health issues and lived in Bothell, then Bellevue, and later Snohomish, all in Washington State. But we kept in touch over the years.

When Betty's cancer reappeared, John and Agnes reached out to us, assuring us of their prayers. Then when John also got cancer, we remained connected by e-mails and letters and prayed for them. Betty was called home to be with the Lord in 2008. Eight months later, John also lost his battle with cancer and joined her. As old friends, Agnes and I kept in touch by e-mail.

Agnes knew that an editor in Albuquerque had been helping me prepare this book for publication. So one day, she asked, "Did you ever get your book published?"

"No," I replied. "I haven't heard from the editor for over a year, so I don't know what's happened." Later, I learned that she had gone through some personal tragedies.

"Why don't you send your book to me?" Agnes said. "I'll be glad to go over it for you."

Since she's a professional editor, I took her up on the offer, and she used her considerable skills to assist me with it. That's when I learned why some writers and publishers call her "Flawless Lawless"!

As the months passed, we not only conferred regarding the book, but we also comforted each other as we grieved the loss of our spouses. Before long, it became obvious that God was moving us into a closer relationship, and we fell in love. Although we hadn't seen each other in seventeen years, we had the firm foundation of a long-time friendship. Since I had just had shoulder surgery, I couldn't travel to see her. So I proposed by phone, and she accepted.

At the time, I was living with my daughter, Kathleen, and her husband, James, in Delaware. When I told Kathleen about our engagement, she said, "But Dad! What if you can't stand each other when you get together? She needs to come here!" I wasn't the least bit worried, but at Kathleen's urging, Agnes flew out to visit us for two weeks. Kathleen picked her up at the airport, and when Agnes walked into the kitchen, I looked her over and said, "Wow!" We joyfully made plans to get married.

Our wedding took place on May 22, 2010, at her church in Snohomish, Washington. Before the service, the pastor told us, "I've never married anyone this old before."

I replied, "I haven't, either!"

Over 125 people gathered from California, Oregon, and British Columbia, along with my family, who came from Delaware, Colorado, and Mexico. We were especially delighted to have many old-time Wycliffe friends attend, some of whom we hadn't seen for years. They had so much fun visiting that one of them quipped, "We ought to do this more often!"

During the final days of Betty and John's lives, they both expressed the wish that the spouses they were leaving behind would find godly companions. Grieving the impending loss of our loved ones at the time, neither Agnes nor I were interested in the notion. But it seemed that God had other ideas.

Now, we like to think of Betty and John peering over heaven's banisters and rejoicing that we can spend our golden years together as co-laborers for Christ, continuing the work that we all began over fifty years ago.

# About the Authors

Richard Elkins graduated from Westmont College. In 1985 he and his wife Betty were named alumni of the year—the first ever to receive that honor from Westmont. Richard later earned a PhD from the University of Hawaii in linguistics and anthropology. He spent forty years as a Wycliffe Bible translator among the Western Bukidnon Manobo people in the Philippines and translated the Manobo New Testament and edited the Manobo Old Testament. He later was the missions' professor at Albuquerque Bible College for ten years and has served as an international translation consultant.

Richard is the author/editor of *The Manobo-English Dictionary* and is the translator/editor of *A Voice from the Hills: Essays on the Culture and Worldview of the Western Bukidnon Manobo People,* which won a national book award in the Philippines. His chapter, "Biblical Inspiration and Bible Translation" is in Willis and Masters' book, *Basic Theology Applied* (Victor Books). His forty-seven linguistic and cultural articles have appeared in such journals as *Ethnology; RELC Anthology,* and *Missiology: An International Review.*

Agnes Lawless Elkins graduated from Prairie Bible College and Seattle Pacific University and did graduate work at Syracuse University in religious journalism. She also studied at the University of North Dakota and Hartford Seminary. Under the name of Agnes Lawless, she authored or coauthored nine books, including *The Drift into Deception* (Kregel); *Captivated by God* (Gospel Light); and *Under His Wings: Protected by God in China* (Christian Growth Ministries). She has had numerous articles published and is the assistant editor of *The Northwest Christian Author.* She also copyedits and proofreads for publishers and individuals. Agnes and her late husband, John Lawless, worked with Wycliffe Bible Translators in the Philippines in the 1950s and 1960s. The Elkinses live in Snohomish, Washington.

# Bibliography

Elkins, Richard E. "The *Anit* Taboo: A Manobo Cultural Unit." *Practical Anthropology* 11:185-188, 1964.

_____. "Biblical Inspiration and Bible Translation." In *Basic Theology Applied: A Practical Application of Basic Theology in Honor of Charles C. Ryrie and His Work,* edited by John and Janet Master and Wesley and Elaine Willis. Colorado Springs, CO: Victor Books, 1995.

_____. "Blood Sacrifice and the Dynamics of Supernatural Power Among the Manobo of Mindanao: Some Missiological Implications." *Missiology: An International Review* XXI, no. 3, July 1993.

_____. "Conversion or Acculturation? A Study of Culture Change and Its Effect on Evangelism in Mindanao Indigenous Societies." *Missiology: An International Review* XXII, no. 2, April 1994.

_____. "Culture Change in a Philippine Folk Society." *Philippine Sociological Review* 14:160-166, 1966.

_____. "Developing Indigenous Leadership." *Notes on Scripture in Use* 13:11-17, Summer Institute of Linguistics, 1987.

_____. "An Extended Proto-Manobo Word List." In *Panagani, Language Planning, Implementation, and Evaluation: Essays in Honor of Bonifacio P. Sibayan on His Sixty-Seventh Birthday*, edited by Andrew B. Gonzales, FSC. Manila: Linguistic Society of the Philippines, 1984.

_____. *Manobo-English Dictionary.* Honolulu: University of Hawaii Press, 1968.

_____. "Translating the New Testament into Manobo." *Kinaadman* XV 2: 65-85, 1993.

_____. "Worldview Constraints on Conversion in an Animistic Society." *Alpha Beta Gamma* II, no. 2, July 2001.

Nelson, Lincoln D. *With Scalpel and the Sword: An American Doctor's Odyssey in the Philippines.* New Cumberland, PA: ABWE Publishing, 1997.

Polenda, Francisco Col-om. *A Voice from the Hills: Essays on the Culture and Worldview of the Western Bukidnon Manobo People*, translated and edited by Richard E. Elkins. Manila: Linguistic Society of the Philippines; Summer Institute of Linguistics, 1989, 2002.

_____. "*Ulegingen:* A Prose Retelling of a Mindanao Epic," translated and edited by Richard E. Elkins. *Kinaadman* XVI 2: 100-225, 1994.

Zorc, R. David Paul. *Proto Philippine Finder List.* Ithaca, NY: Cornell University, 1971.

Also by Richard E. Elkins:

*Manobo-English Dictionary*

*A Voice from the Hills: Essays on the Culture and Worldview of the Western Bukidnon Manobo*, translated and edited

Also by Agnes C. Lawless:

*A Place for God to Live: A Blueprint for Christian Living Pictured in the Tabernacle*

*The Word: God's Manual for Maturity*, with Eadie Goodboy

*The Drift into Deception: The Eight Characteristics of Abusive Christianity*, with John W. Lawless

*Under His Wings: Protected by God in China*

*Keys to God's Heart: Unlocking Leviticus*, with Harriet Salathe

*Captivated by God*, with Eadie Goodboy